1 *MEALS IN MINUTES* 6

2 *BUDGET MEALS* 24

3 *COOK AHEAD, SAVE TIME* 44

4 *REAL FOOD FOR KIDS* 62

5 *HEALTHY AND LIGHT* 76

6 *VEGETARIAN DELIGHTS* 92

7 *EASY GOURMET FOOD* 110

STOCK CUBES

Original

Chicken

Vegetable

HERB & SPICE CUBES

Chinese

Indian

Mexican

Italian

CRUMBLE IN THE CUBES

Welcome to *The New Oxo Cookbook*.

It's a different sort of cookbook. Oxo have thought long and hard about all the different demands that we face in getting meals on the table and each chapter in *The New Oxo Cookbook* is packed with simple and delicious recipes, which meet a particular need – whether it be for speedy suppers, balanced meals for hungry kids or tasty recipes for anyone trying to keep their calorie intake low.

The easy-to-follow recipes are clearly laid out and each is accompanied by a mouth-watering photograph. There are lots of handy tips from Oxo's many years of experience of home cooking, and easy-reference symbols that form an instant guide to cooking times, serving quantities, which dishes can be microwaved or frozen, and, where appropriate, calorie counts.

You'll find recipes here for vegetarian meals – but it's not a vegetarian cookbook; you'll find recipes that could easily come from a special occasion cookbook – but it's a great deal

The

New OXO
Cookbook

Published in Great Britain by
Simon & Schuster
A Paramount Communications
Company
Copyright © 1994, Brooke Bond
Foods Ltd

Simon & Schuster Ltd
West Garden Place
Kendal Street
London W2 2AQ

First published 1994
Paperback edition 1995

A CIP catalogue record is available
from the British Library
ISBN 0-85941-877-4
Printed in Great Britain

CONTENTS

more than that. In fact you'll find every sort of recipe that today's busy meal providers need – whether you're a reluctant conscript to the kitchen or an enthusiastic amateur cook.

The New Oxo Cookbook offers lots of new ideas which use both the Oxo stock cubes (Original, Chicken and Vegetable) and the new range of Herb & Spice cubes. There are four flavours to choose from – Chinese, Italian, Indian and Mexican. You can use them to give ethnic recipes an authentic flavour, or to add a little extra interest to more traditional everyday dishes. And nothing could be simpler. Forget about assembling a great collection of bottles and jars from the backs of cupboards and shelves and discovering that, even then, you haven't got all the spices you need – Oxo have done it all for you – you just crumble in the cubes.

The New Oxo Cookbook is the sort of cookbook that will soon become as vital a piece of equipment in your kitchen as your pots and pans – the sort of cookbook, in fact, that you'll find yourself referring to day after day, meal after meal.

KEY TO

Number of servings

Approximate cooking time
1 hr 25 mins

Approximate calories per serving
235

Suitable for microwave cooking

Suitable for freezing

MEALS IN MINUTES

There are all sorts of reasons – work, family commitments, leisure activities – why most of us have very little time to spend in the kitchen. But with only minutes to spare it is still possible to prepare delicious meals. The trick here is to choose quick-cooking ingredients, such as pasta, fish, chicken and turkey, and then to create interesting dishes with a few handy shortcuts from Oxo.

'A sprinkling of fresh parsley would enhance the presentation.'

7

Pork Amandine

Serve this creamy pork dish with freshly cooked pasta or rice.

225 g / 8 oz pork fillet (tenderloin)
225 g / 8 oz button mushrooms
I garlic clove
25 g / I oz flaked almonds
15 g / ½ oz butter
2 Oxo Italian Herb & Spice cubes
150 ml / ¼ pt double cream
freshly ground pepper

I Cut the pork into very thin slices. Wash, dry and slice or quarter the mushrooms. Skin and crush the garlic.

2 Put the almonds in a large non-stick frying pan and cook over high heat, stirring constantly, until golden brown. Remove them from the pan.

3 Heat the butter in the pan and add the pork. Cook over high heat, stirring frequently, until the meat is well browned on both sides.

4 Reduce the heat to medium-high and add the garlic and mushrooms. Cook, stirring constantly, for 3–4 minutes.

5 Crumble the Italian Herb & Spice cubes into the cream and stir well. Add to the pan and cook for 5 minutes or until bubbling hot, stirring frequently. Season with pepper. Serve sprinkled with the almonds.

OXO Tip
If the pork is put in the freezer for an hour before using, it is much easier to cut it into paper-thin slices.

Meals in Minutes

8

Meals in Minutes 9

Sizzling Spicy Beef with Peppers

This is a really speedy dish. Serve it with egg noodles which can be prepared in the time it takes to cook the spicy beef.

350 g / 12 oz lean rump steak
1 Oxo Mexican Herb & Spice cube
10 ml / 2 tsp cornflour
1 Original Oxo cube
1 medium onion
1 red pepper
1 yellow pepper
4 spring onions
45 ml / 3 tbsp oil

1 Cut the steak into thin strips and put the strips in a dish. Crumble the Mexican Herb & Spice cube and mix it with the cornflour. Add the mixture to the beef and toss everything together. Crumble the Original Oxo cube into 150 ml / ¼ pt boiling water.

2 Peel and thinly slice the onion. Remove core and seeds from the peppers and slice. Trim the spring onions and chop.

3 Heat 15 ml / 1 tbsp oil in a large frying pan, add the onion and peppers and sauté for 3–4 minutes over a high heat until the onions are golden. Remove from the pan and set aside.

4 Heat the remaining oil, add the beef and cook over maximum heat until sizzling and browned.

5 Return the vegetables to the pan, pour in the stock and simmer for 2 minutes. Serve garnished with the chopped spring onion.

OXO *Tip*
Try this recipe with lean pork fillet or skinless chicken breasts instead of beef.

Flash-Fry Steaks with Sherried Mushrooms

1 small onion
1 Original Oxo cube
60 ml / 4 tbsp dry sherry
2 flash-fry steaks
175 g / 6 oz button mushrooms
5 ml / 1 tsp oil
60 ml / 4 tbsp crème fraîche
freshly ground pepper

1 Peel and slice the onion very thinly. Crumble the Original Oxo cube into 150 ml / ¼ pt boiling water. Stir in the sherry.

2 Heat half the oil in a large non-stick frying pan. Add the steaks and cook for 2–3 minutes on each side, depending on their thickness. Remove from the pan and keep hot.

3 Add the remaining oil to the pan and stir in the onion and mushrooms. Cook over medium-high heat for 2–3 minutes. Add the stock to the pan and cook for 5 minutes, stirring once or twice, until reduced by half.

4 Gradually add the crème fraîche to the mixture, stirring until the sauce is smooth. Season with pepper.

5 Serve the mushrooms with the steaks.

Tex-Mex Pasta

Chorizos are small spicy sausages. You should be able to find them easily on good delicatessen counters.

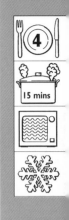

I medium onion
I clove garlic
150 g / 5 oz chorizo sausage
350 g / 12 oz tagliatelle
15 ml / I tbsp sunflower oil
397 g can chopped tomatoes
I Oxo Mexican Herb & Spice cube
15 ml / I tbsp tomato purée
397 g can red kidney or cannellini beans
100 g / 4 oz frozen sweetcorn
50 g / 2 oz grated Cheddar cheese

I Peel and chop the onion. Peel and then crush or finely chop the garlic. Cut the sausage into 0.5 cm / ¼ in slices.

2 Cook the pasta in a large pan of boiling salted water until just tender. Meanwhile, heat the oil in another pan, add the onion and garlic and cook for 4–5 minutes until softened.

3 Add the chopped tomatoes, crumble in the Mexican Herb & Spice cube and then stir in all the remaining ingredients except the cheese. Allow to simmer for 8 minutes.

4 Drain the pasta and divide it between four dishes. Spoon over the spicy sauce and top with grated cheese before serving.

Meals in Minutes

13

Chicken and Asparagus Pasta

Watch pasta carefully to make sure it cooks to just the right stage. Italians say it should be 'al dente' which means 'firm to the bite.' It should be tender, but not soft and mushy.

100–150 g / 4–5 oz chicken breast
4 spring onions
225 g / 8 oz asparagus
I Chicken Oxo cube
I Oxo Italian Herb & Spice cube
100 g / 4 oz pasta quills
5 ml / I tsp oil
15 g / ½ oz butter
15 ml / I tbsp plain flour
75 ml / 3 fl oz milk
freshly ground pepper
15 ml / I tbsp freshly grated
    Parmesan cheese

I Slice the chicken breast thinly. Chop the spring onions. Cut the tips off the asparagus and put to one side. Slice the remaining asparagus stalks. Crumble the Chicken and Italian Herb & Spice cubes into 150 ml / ¼ pt boiling water.

2 Cook the pasta in plenty of boiling salted water until just tender.

3 Meanwhile, heat the oil and butter in a non-stick frying pan and cook the chicken over a medium-high heat until golden brown and cooked through. Remove from the pan and keep hot.

4 Add the onions and asparagus stalks to the pan and stir, off the heat, for 1–2 minutes. Stir in the flour, then gradually add the milk, stirring continuously. Add the stock.

5 Cook, stirring, until the sauce boils and thickens. Add the asparagus tips, season with pepper and cook for 2 minutes. Add the chicken.

6 Drain the pasta and add to the pan. Lightly toss together and serve in warmed bowls, sprinkled with Parmesan cheese.

OXO Tip
If you prefer you can make shavings of Parmesan cheese, instead of grating it. Use a potato peeler and cut the cheese very thinly.

Italian Chicken and Bacon Salad

Serve with crusty bread for a tasty main-meal salad. You can use any variety of lettuce that is available.

3 boneless, skinless chicken breasts
5 rashers lean back bacon
4 tomatoes
½ cucumber
a bunch of spring onions
2 Oxo Italian Herb & Spice cubes
a large bag of prepared salad leaves
60 ml / 4 tbsp olive oil
15 ml / 1 tbsp red wine vinegar

1 Cut the chicken and bacon into thin strips. Cut the tomatoes into wedges. Slice or dice the cucumber and then trim and chop the spring onions.

2 Put the chicken into a dish and crumble over the 2 Italian Herb & Spice cubes. Toss everything together so the chicken is coated with the mixture.

3 Put the salad leaves into a large serving bowl, add the tomatoes, cucumber and spring onions.

4 Heat half of the oil in a large frying pan, add the chicken and bacon and cook for 8 minutes, stirring, until the chicken is lightly golden brown.

5 Lift the chicken from the pan and add to the salad.

6 Put the remaining oil into the pan and add the vinegar. Swirl around and mix with the pan juices. Then pour over the salad and toss together. Serve immediately.

OXO Tip
Wash and dry the lettuce leaves carefully to prevent the salad becoming soggy and then the warm dressing will coat everything evenly.

Chicken and Vegetable Stir Fry

350 g / 12 oz boneless chicken
  breasts
2 celery sticks
I medium carrot
2.5 cm / I in piece of root ginger
  or 2.5 ml / ½ tsp ground ginger
I medium red pepper
I medium yellow pepper
I medium courgette
I bunch spring onions
227 g can water chestnuts
3 Oxo Chinese Herb & Spice cubes
60 ml / 4 tbsp dry sherry
15 ml / I tbsp oil

1 Skin and thinly slice the chicken. Trim and slice the celery diagonally. Peel and cut the carrot into thin sticks. Peel and grate the root ginger. Halve the peppers, discarding the stem and seeds, and slice into strips. Slice the courgette. Trim and slice the spring onions, diagonally. Drain the can of water chestnuts. Crumble 2 Chinese Herb & Spice cubes into the sherry.

2 Heat the oil in a wok and add the chicken. Crumble over 1 Chinese Herb & Spice cube. Cook over a high heat, stirring, until the chicken is light golden brown.

3 Add the celery, carrot and ginger and cook, stirring, for 1 minute. Add the peppers and courgette and cook, stirring, for 1 minute.

4 Add the spring onions, water chestnuts and sherry mixture. Cook, stirring, for 1 minute. Serve immediately.

Chinese Chicken Noodle Soup

A filling soup that is a meal in itself. Eat it at once – if it is left to stand the noodles become soggy. Try using prawns instead of chicken – you will need 100 g / 4 oz of peeled prawns.

225 g / 8 oz skinless chicken
100 g / 4 oz button mushrooms
1 red pepper
15 ml / 1 tbsp oil
1 Chicken Oxo cube
3 Oxo Chinese Herb & Spice cubes
75 g / 3 oz frozen sweetcorn
75 g / 3 oz thread egg noodles
5 spring onions

1 Cut the chicken into small, thin strips. Slice the mushrooms. Remove the core and seeds from the pepper and chop it into small dice.

2 Heat the oil in a saucepan. Add the mushrooms and sauté for 2 minutes. Pour in 1.1 litres / 2 pt of boiling water and then crumble in the Chicken and Chinese Herb & Spice cubes.

3 Bring to the boil, stir in the chicken, pepper and sweetcorn and simmer for 5 minutes.

4 Break up the noodles, add to the pan and simmer for a further 3 minutes. Trim and thinly slice the spring onions. Stir them into the soup and then let the soup stand for 2 minutes before serving.

Turkey Escalopes with Orange and Rosemary

Serve the turkey with new potatoes and a green vegetable. If you cook this recipe in a microwave, use a browning dish.

2 large oranges
8 small turkey steaks/fillets
    weighing approximately
    550 g / 1¼ lb
25 g / 1 oz seasoned flour
1 small onion
1 Chicken Oxo cube
30 ml / 2 tbsp sunflower oil
5 ml / 1 tsp fresh rosemary
salt and freshly ground pepper

1 Grate the rind from one of the oranges and set aside. Peel the orange and cut into segments. Cut the segments in half. Squeeze the juice from the second orange.

2 Place each turkey steak between cling film and beat with a rolling pin to a thickness of 0.5 cm /¼ in. Coat each side with seasoned flour.

3 Peel and chop the onion finely. Crumble the Chicken cube into 240 ml / 8 fl oz boiling water.

4 Heat half the oil in a large non-stick frying pan. Add as many turkey steaks as will fit into the pan and cook over a medium high heat for 2–3 minutes on each side until golden. Keep warm while cooking the rest. Add the rest of the oil as it is needed.

5 Add the onion to the pan. Pour in the stock, orange juice and grated rind. Finely chop the rosemary and add to the pan. Simmer for about 5 minutes until reduced by about one-third.

6 Add the orange segments and heat them through. Season the sauce if necessary and then serve the turkey escalopes with the sauce poured over.

OXO Tip
Turkey breast meat is perfect as part of a healthy diet. It is low in fat and calories. If the steaks are large, allow one per serving and cut each one in half before flattening the pieces out.

10 mins

Fried Fish with Lemon Sauce

Serve with noodles.

2 Oxo Chinese Herb & Spice cubes
350 g / 12 oz skinned white fish
fillets, such as plaice
10 ml / 2 tsp + 30 ml / 2 tbsp
cornflour
5 ml / 1 tsp sugar
15 ml / 1 tbsp dry sherry
15 ml / 1 tbsp light soy sauce
juice of ½ lemon
4 spring onions
15 ml / 1 tbsp oil

1 Crumble 1 Chinese Herb & Spice cube over the fish and then cut the fish into finger-size strips. Leave it to stand for about 15 minutes.

2 Meanwhile, mix the 10 ml / 2 tsp of cornflour with the sugar, sherry, soy sauce and lemon juice. Crumble in the remaining Chinese Herb & Spice cube. Slice the spring onions diagonally.

3 Coat the fish strips with the remaining cornflour, shaking off any excess.

4 Heat the oil in a non-stick wok or frying pan and fry the fish quickly, a few strips at a time, until golden brown. Lift them out and keep warm.

5 Add the onions to the pan and cook for 1 minute, stirring. Add the sauce mixture and bring to the boil, stirring. Slide the fish into the sauce and serve immediately.

Quick Spiced Fish

This is made in minutes with Herb & Spice cubes, so there's no need to fiddle around with spices yourself. Serve with boiled rice.

12 mins

300 g / 10 oz skinless cod or haddock fillet
225 g / 8 oz leeks
100 g / 4 oz baby button mushrooms
1 red, yellow or green pepper
15 ml / 1 tbsp sunflower oil
2 Oxo Indian Herb & Spice cubes

1 Cut the fish into chunks. Halve the leeks lengthwise and cut into thick slices. Wash and drain them well. Trim the mushrooms. Remove the core and seeds from the pepper and cut it into dice.

2 Heat the oil in a non-stick frying pan and add the fish. Crumble over 1 Indian Herb & Spice cube and sauté gently for 4–5 minutes. Carefully lift the fish out of the pan with a slotted spoon.

3 Turn up the heat and add the vegetables and second Indian Herb & Spice cube to the pan. Stir-fry the vegetables for 5 minutes until just tender.

4 Return the fish and the juices to the pan and heat everything together gently, taking care not to break up the fish too much.

Meals in Minutes

23

BUDGET MEALS

Forget the dull image budget cooking has had in the past – it can be very satisfying to create a delicious meal from inexpensive ingredients. The recipes in this chapter use the Herb & Spice cubes to make international dishes *with* the authentic flavours of the originals, but *without* the hassle of buying lots of individual little jars and packets (very often the spices inside go stale before you can use them up). These dishes are all easy to prepare and would be ideal for students or young people cooking for themselves on a limited budget.

'There's more if you want it.'
'I might just stay longer then.'

Lamb Pasticcio

This Mediterranean dish can be made with minced beef, but lamb makes a nice change. Serve with green salad.

I large onion
2 cloves garlic
15 ml / I tbsp olive oil
450 g / I lb minced lamb
3 Oxo Italian Herb & Spice cubes
I Original Oxo cube
2.5 ml / ½ tsp ground cinnamon
60 ml / 4 tbsp tomato purée
a pinch of sugar
100 g / 4 oz frozen leaf spinach, thawed
Topping:
100 g / 4 oz pasta twists
2 eggs
25 g / I oz butter
25 g / I oz flour
450 ml / ¾ pt warm milk
50 g / 2 oz grated Cheddar cheese
salt and freshly ground pepper

I Peel and chop the onion. Peel and crush the garlic. Heat the oil in a large frying pan, add the onion and cook until golden.

2 Add the garlic and lamb and cook over a high heat until the lamb is browned.

3 Crumble in 2 Italian Herb & Spice cubes. Add the Original Oxo cube to 300 ml / ½ pt water and pour into the pan. Add the cinnamon, tomato purée and sugar, and simmer uncovered for 25 minutes. Drain the spinach and stir into the meat.

4 Heat the oven to 190°C/350°F/mark 5. Meanwhile bring a medium size saucepan of water to the boil. Crumble in the third Italian Herb & Spice cube and add the pasta. Cook until just tender. Drain.

5 Beat the eggs. Melt the butter in the pan, add the flour and cook over a low heat for 1 minute. Remove the pan from the heat, and gradually add the milk. Bring to the boil, stirring all the time and then simmer for 2 minutes.

6 Off the heat stir the cheese into the sauce. Then stir in the eggs and then the pasta. Season with salt and pepper.

7 Season the meat mixture and then turn into an ovenproof dish. Spoon over the pasta mixture. Bake for 30–35 minutes until golden.

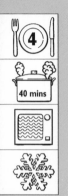

Tuna and Pasta Bake

Use a mix of different coloured pasta for this dish and try out different shapes and varieties each time you make it. Serve with a green salad.

2 Oxo Italian Herb & Spice cubes
225 g / 8 oz pasta
175 g / 6 oz broccoli florets
25 g / 1 oz butter
25 g / 1 oz flour
450 ml / ¾ pt warm milk
100 g / 4 oz grated Cheddar cheese
200 g / 7 oz can tuna in brine

1 Put a large pan of water on to boil, crumble in 1 Italian Herb & Spice cube and then add the pasta. Cook for 8–10 minutes until the pasta is tender, but still retains a little 'bite' – this is what the Italians call 'al dente'. Drain the pasta.

2 Meanwhile, preheat the oven to 190°C/375°F/mark 5. Put a smaller pan of water on to boil. When it is boiling, blanch the broccoli in it for 3 minutes and then drain.

3 Melt the butter in a saucepan, add the flour and cook over a low heat for 1 minute. Take the pan off the heat and gradually add the milk. Slowly bring to a simmer and cook for 2 minutes. Crumble in the second Italian Herb & Spice cube and add 75 g /3 oz of the cheese.

4 Drain the tuna and break into large flakes. Add to the sauce with the pasta and broccoli. Turn into a greased ovenproof dish.

5 Scatter over the remaining cheese and bake in the oven for 20 minutes until golden on top.

OXO Tip
Adding 1 or 2 Herb & Spice cubes to pasta during cooking gives it a delicious taste which will enhance any sauce.

8 mins

Chinese Noodles with Omelette Rolls

1 red pepper
1 bunch of spring onions
2 Oxo Chinese Herb & Spice cubes
15 ml / 1 tbsp light soy sauce
150 g / 5 oz medium egg noodles
2 eggs
30 ml / 2 tbsp oil
100 g / 4 oz peeled prawns

1 Halve the pepper, remove the core and thinly slice. Trim the spring onions and chop. Crumble 1 Chinese Herb & Spice cube into the soy sauce.

2 Bring a saucepan of water to the boil, add the noodles and then remove from the heat and set aside for 6 minutes.

3 Beat the eggs. Heat 15 ml / 1 tbsp of the oil in a 23 cm / 9 in frying pan, add the eggs and cook until set. Slide out onto a board and roll up.

4 Heat the remaining oil in a large frying pan or wok. Add the pepper, spring onion and prawns. Crumble in the second Chinese Herb & Spice cube and stir fry for 3 minutes.

5 Drain the noodles and put them back in the saucepan. Toss with the soy sauce. Add to the wok and toss together for 2 minutes. Divide between 2 warm plates.

6 Cut the rolled omelette into slices and arrange over the noodles.

Budget Meals

30

Bombay Potatoes

Grating the onion and potatoes is easy if you use a food processor. These must be eaten at once while the outside is still crispy. Serve with grilled tomatoes and mushrooms.

1 medium onion
1 kg / 2 lb potatoes
6 eggs
2 Oxo Indian Herb & Spice cubes
50 g / 2 oz plain flour
salt and freshly ground pepper
oil for frying

1 Finely grate the onion. Peel and coarsely grate the potatoes. Squeeze as much moisture out as possible. Beat 2 eggs with the crumbled Indian Herb & Spice cubes.

2 Combine the onion with the potatoes, beaten egg mixture and flour. Season the mixture.

3 Heat 1 cm / ½ in of oil in a frying pan. To make the pancakes, drop 1 heaped tablespoon of mixture into the pan and fry for 3–4 minutes for each side. You should be able to make about three at a time. When golden and crisp on each side, drain them on kitchen paper. Keep warm while cooking the rest of the mixture. The mixture makes 12 pancakes.

4 In a separate pan fry the remaining eggs. Allow 3 pancakes per serving, topped with a fried egg.

1 hr 30 mins

Jacket Potatoes with Mustard Sausage Topping

Here is a delicious topping made with sausages, onions, mushrooms and a mustard sauce.

four 225–275 g / 8–10 oz baking
  potatoes
1 medium onion
75 g / 3 oz button mushrooms
15 ml / 1 tbsp oil
225 g / 8 oz chipolata sausages
1 Chicken Oxo cube
15 ml / 1 tbsp wholegrain mustard
5 ml / 1 tsp cornflour
15 ml / 1 tsp chopped parsley

1 Heat the oven to 190°C / 375°F / mark 5. Scrub the potatoes and prick them with a fork or the point of a sharp knife. Place them on the oven shelf and bake for 1½ hours, turning once.

2 Meanwhile peel and slice the onion. Slice the mushrooms.

3 Heat the oil in a medium size frying pan. Add the sausages and cook until browned all over. Remove them and set aside.

4 Cook the onions in the pan until golden, add the mushrooms and cook for a few moments more. Crumble the Chicken cube into 240 ml / 8 fl oz boiling water. Pour all but 30 ml / 2 tbsp of it into the pan and bring to a simmer.

5 Cut the sausages into three, return them to the pan and stir in the mustard. Simmer for 10 minutes.

6 Blend the cornflour with the reserved stock. Add it to the pan and simmer to thicken.

7 Cut a cross in the tops of the potatoes and then press the sides together, making them look nice and fluffy. Spoon over the sausage filling and garnish with chopped parsley.

OXO Tip
For speedy spuds, cook potatoes in the microwave. Arrange them on kitchen paper and cook on FULL POWER for 15–20 minutes (depending on the size of the potatoes). Turn them over halfway. Leave to stand for 5 minutes, then split open and fill.

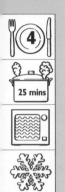

Baked Chilli Peppers

The flavour of the smoked Cheddar cheese goes particularly well with the spiced meat filling, but a mature Cheddar could be used instead. Use two Oxo Mexican Herb & Spice cubes for a very spicy flavour. Serve with a salad of sliced tomatoes and cucumber.

4 large red, green and / or yellow peppers
1 medium onion
5 ml / 1 tsp oil
1–2 Oxo Mexican Herb & Spice cubes
45 ml / 3 tbsp tomato purée
350 g / 12 oz extra lean minced beef
100 g / 4 oz soft cheese with herbs and garlic
50 g / 2 oz smoked Cheddar cheese

1 Slice off one-third of each pepper, leaving the stalk attached. Remove the seeds and pith from each portion.

2 Place the larger portions in a saucepan, cover with cold water and bring to the boil. Reduce the heat and simmer for 3 minutes. Drain well.

3 Meanwhile, finely chop the remaining portions of each pepper. Peel and finely chop the onion.

4 Heat the oil in a large non-stick frying pan and add the chopped peppers and onion. Cover and cook over medium-high heat until soft.

5 Crumble over the Mexican Herb & Spice cube(s) and add the tomato purée. Stir well. Crumble the minced beef into the pan.

6 Increase the heat to high and cook, stirring frequently, until the meat is no longer pink. Remove from the heat and stir in the soft cheese.

7 Arrange the peppers in an ovenproof dish. Spoon in the meat filling, shaping to a smooth rounded top. Thinly slice the cheese and arrange on top of the peppers.

8 Add 300 ml / 2 tbsp water to the bottom of the ovenproof dish. Cook at 200°C / 400°F / mark 6 for 15 minutes until golden brown.

OXO Tip
Try using minced turkey instead of beef.

30 mins

Summer Vegetable Pie

This is an excellent recipe to make in the summer when peppers are plentiful and inexpensive. Serve with a mixed green salad.

225 g / 8 oz frozen puff pastry, defrosted
I egg
I Spanish onion
2 cloves garlic
I large courgette
I red pepper
I yellow pepper
30 ml / 2 tbsp olive oil
I Oxo Italian Herb & Spice cube
2 tbsp freshly grated Parmesan cheese

I On a lightly floured surface, roll out the pastry to a rectangle 28 × 25.5 cm / 11 × 10 in, and transfer to a greased baking tray. Beat the egg and brush a 2.5 cm / 1 in border around the edges. Fold over the edges on all sides to form a 1 cm / ½ in border and brush with the egg. With a blunt knife mark the border with diagonal lines. Prick the inside of the pastry case with a fork and refrigerate for 30 minutes.

2 Meanwhile, peel and slice the onion. Peel and slice the garlic. Dice the courgette and remove the core and seeds from the peppers and cut them into 2.5 cm / 1 in squares.

3 Heat the oven to 200°C / 400°F / mark 6.

4 Heat the oil in a large frying pan. Add the onion and cook over a medium high heat for about 10 minutes until soft and golden. Add the rest of the vegetables and continue to cook for a further 10 minutes until the vegetables begin to soften. Crumble over the Italian Herb & Spice cube and stir together.

5 While the vegetables are cooking, scatter the base of the pastry with the Parmesan and place in the oven for 10 minutes. Then, remove from the oven and press down the centre. Add the vegetables. Return the pie to the oven and continue to cook for 10 minutes until the edges are crisp and golden. Eat it while it is hot.

OXO Tip

You could add some mushrooms to the vegetables but be sure to fry them until all their liquor has evaporated, otherwise it will seep into the pastry.

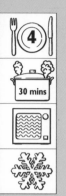

Sausage Goulash

Look out for good quality sausages for this recipe. This makes a super family meal as most children enjoy sausages. Serve it with potatoes – either creamed or jacket – or pasta.

I large onion
2 large carrots
I Original Oxo cube
15 ml / I tbsp oil
450 g / I lb coarse pork sausages
15 ml / I tbsp paprika
15 ml / I tbsp flour
397 g can chopped tomatoes
2.5 ml / ½ tsp dried herbs
a pinch of sugar
salt and freshly ground pepper
chopped parsley, to garnish

I Peel and thickly slice the onion. Peel and slice the carrots. Crumble the Original Oxo cube into 300 ml / ½ pt boiling water.

2 Heat the oil in a large flameproof casserole, add the sausages and fry for about 5 minutes until browned all over. Remove the sausages from the pan and cut each sausage in half.

3 Add the onion and carrot to the pan and cook gently until golden – about 6–8 minutes. Stir in the paprika and flour and then pour in the stock and tomatoes. Bring to the boil and simmer.

4 Stir in the herbs and sugar. Return the sausages to the pan, and then cover and simmer for 15 minutes until the sausages are cooked through. Season if necessary and garnish with the chopped parsley.

OXO Tip
With so many different and delicious varieties of sausage available, it's well worth trying out a new type or flavour in your goulash.

Fragrant Chinese Meatballs

Accompany this dish with Chinese egg noodles.

227 g can water chestnuts
1 bunch of spring onions
450 g / 1 lb minced pork
2 Oxo Chinese Herb & Spice cubes
175 g / 6 oz beansprouts
1 red pepper
45 ml / 3 tbsp oil
30 ml / 2 tbsp light soy sauce

1 Drain and finely chop the water chestnuts. Trim 4 spring onions and chop them finely. Put the spring onions and the water chestnuts in a bowl with the pork, crumble in the Chinese Herb & Spice cubes and mix together.

2 Divide the mixture into 24 and roll into balls.

3 Wash the beansprouts. Remove the core and seeds from the pepper and cut into thin slices. Shred the remaining spring onions.

4 Heat 2 tablespoons of the oil in a large frying pan, add the pork balls and cook over a medium heat for 8–10 minutes, turning them all the time until they are browned. Lift from the pan and keep warm.

5 Add the rest of the oil to the pan. Add the prepared vegetables and stir fry over a high heat for 2 minutes. Pour in the soy sauce. Combine with the vegetables and then serve with meatballs.

Bacon Chops
with Mushroom Sauce

If bacon chops are unavailable, buy small gammon steaks.

1 small onion
2 cloves garlic
225 g / 8 oz mushrooms
1 Chicken Oxo cube
4 bacon chops (approximately
    150 g / 5 oz each)
40 g / 1½ oz butter
30 ml / 2 tbsp medium sherry
10 ml / 2 tsp cornflour
chopped parsley to garnish

1 Peel and slice the onion. Peel and finely chop the garlic. Trim and slice the mushrooms. Crumble the Chicken cube into 300 ml / ½ pt boiling water. Place the chops on a grill pan and preheat the grill.

2 Melt the butter in a saucepan. Brush a little of the butter over the chops and then place the chops under a medium hot grill to cook for 3–4 minutes on each side.

3 Add the onion, garlic and mushrooms to the butter in the pan and cook over a high heat for 4–5 minutes until golden.

4 Add the stock and sherry and simmer for 3 minutes. Blend the cornflour with a little water, add to the pan and simmer to thicken.

5 Serve the chops with the sauce. Garnish with chopped parsley.

Budget Meals

41

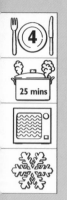

Chicken Creole

Chicken thighs are an economical cut of chicken. If you are in a hurry use ready-skinned and boned thighs. Serve with rice or jacket potatoes.

8 chicken thighs
I small onion
I clove garlic
I green pepper
15 ml / I tbsp oil
397 g can chopped tomatoes
2 Oxo Mexican Herb & Spice cubes
15 ml / I tbsp tomato purée
5 ml / I tsp sugar
2.5 ml / ½ tsp dried thyme
2.5 ml / ½ tsp dried basil
salt

1 Remove the skin from the chicken thighs, cut out the bone and then chop the flesh into 2.5 cm / 1 in pieces. Peel and slice the onion. Peel and crush the garlic. Remove the core and seeds from the pepper and cut it into dice.

2 Heat the oil in a non-stick frying pan, add the chicken and sauté until golden. Remove with a slotted spoon and set aside.

3 Add the onion, garlic and pepper to the pan and fry for 3–4 minutes to soften. Stir in the canned tomatoes, crumble in the Mexican Herb & Spice cubes. Return the chicken to the pan and add all the remaining ingredients except for the salt.

4 Simmer for 15 minutes until the chicken is tender and the sauce is thickened. Season with salt if necessary.

OXO Tip
If you are cooking for children you may prefer to add only one Herb & Spice cube and check the sauce for spiciness.

COOK AHEAD, SAVE TIME

The dishes in this chapter are delicious made and eaten the same day, but very often a casserole improves in flavour when made a day ahead and then re-heated. These recipes are ideal to make in advance or in bulk and all have got a special topping or finishing touch to add when you re-heat them to give them just that little extra appeal for family meals.

'Ah... Mum's chops usually come with gravy.'

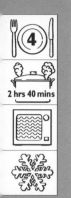

Carbonade of Beef

This is a rich-tasting casserole with crisp bread topping that really livens up the dish. Don't, however, attempt to microwave or freeze the topping. It should be baked in the oven and then served crisp and hot.

2 hrs 40 mins

700 g / 1½ lb braising steak
2 medium onions
15 g / ½ oz butter
15 ml / I tbsp oil
2 cloves garlic
5 ml / I tsp brown sugar
15 ml / I tbsp plain flour
I Original Oxo cube
300 ml / ½ pt stout, e.g. Guinness
I bay leaf
a pinch each of thyme and nutmeg
Topping:
8 slices French bread
15 ml / I tbsp olive oil
I Oxo Italian Herb & Spice cube

1 Heat the oven to 180°C/350°F/mark 4. Cut the meat into 5 cm / 2 in pieces. Peel and slice the onions.

2 Heat the butter and oil in a large frying pan, add the meat and cook until browned all over. Transfer to a large ovenproof casserole.

3 Put the onions into the frying pan and cook for 4–5 minutes to soften. Peel and finely chop the garlic. Add it to the pan with the sugar and cook for 1 minute. Stir in the flour.

4 Crumble the Original Oxo cube into 300 ml / ½ pt boiling water and then add to the pan with the stout. Bring to the boil and transfer to the casserole.

5 Add bay leaf, thyme and nutmeg. Cover the casserole and cook for 2 hours until the meat is tender.

6 Increase oven temperature to 190°C/375°F/mark 5. Brush the slices of bread with the oil. Crumble the Italian Herb & Spice cube over the bread slices and arrange them on top of the casserole. Bake for 20–25 minutes until crisp and golden.

Cook ahead
Prepare as far as the end of stage 5. Cool and refrigerate. Re-heat the casserole and then add the bread topping.

Cook ahead, save time

46

Somerset Beef Pie

You may, if you wish, microwave the filling for this tasty pie, but bake the pastry conventionally in the oven.

1 small onion
1 large carrot
1 large parsnip or 225 g / 8 oz swede
1 large potato
15 ml / 1 tbsp oil
450 g / 1 lb lean minced beef
2 Original Oxo cubes
240 ml / 8 fl oz dry cider
10 ml / 2 tsp cornflour
salt and freshly ground pepper
Pastry:
225 g / 8 oz plain flour
5 ml / 1 tsp mustard powder
50 g / 2 oz butter or margarine
50 g / 2 oz white vegetable fat
75 g / 3 oz mature Cheddar cheese

1 To make the pastry, sift the flour, mustard and a pinch of salt into a bowl. Add the fats and rub in until fine and crumbly. Finely grate the cheese and stir into the mixture.

2 Add 5–6 tablespoons cold water. Mix to form a dough. Turn onto a lightly floured surface. Knead until smooth. Wrap in cling film and refrigerate.

3 Peel and chop the onion. Peel the other vegetables and cut into dice.

4 Heat the oil in a large non-stick frying pan. Add the onion and cook for 3 minutes.

5 Add the beef and cook over a high heat for about 5 minutes, stirring until the beef is browned. Add the vegetables.

6 Crumble the Original Oxo cubes into 150 ml / ¼ pt boiling water then add to the pan with the cider. Cover and allow to simmer for 20–25 minutes until the vegetables are just tender.

7 Blend the cornflour with a little water, add to the pan and simmer until thickened. Season with salt and pepper if necessary. Turn into a 1.1 litres / 2 pt pie dish.

8 Heat the oven to 200°C/400°F/mark 6.

9 Roll out the pastry so that it is larger than the top of your pie dish by a margin of 5 cm / 2 in all the way round. Cut a 2.5 cm / 1 in strip from the outer edge and place this on the dampened rim of the dish. Brush the strip with water and cover with the pastry lid. Press the edges lightly to seal them and trim off any excess pastry.

10 Bake for 25–30 minutes until golden.

Cook ahead

Prepare to the end of step 9. Refrigerate. Allow an extra 15 minutes in the oven at 180°C/350°F/mark 4. During this last 15 minutes cover the top with foil.

Cook ahead, save time

Greek Beef and Pasta Bake

Serve with a green salad and crusty bread for a satisfying, tasty meal. Passata is a smooth, pourable purée of sieved tomatoes. It is sold in jars, cans and bottles and is available from most supermarkets.

700 g / 1½ lb braising steak
1 large onion
2 cloves garlic
60 ml / 4 tbsp olive oil
1 Original Oxo cube
300 ml / ½ pt passata
5 ml / 1 tsp ground cinnamon
5 ml / 1 tsp ground cumin
5 ml / 1 tsp dried oregano
salt and freshly ground pepper
100 g / 4 oz macaroni

1 Heat the oven to 180°C/ 350°F/mark 4. Cut the meat into 4 cm / 1½ in cubes. Peel and chop the onion. Peel and crush the garlic.

2 Heat the oil in a frying pan, add the meat and cook until browned. Transfer to an ovenproof casserole.

3 Put the onion into the frying pan and cook until golden. Add the garlic and cook another minute. Add it to the beef.

4 Crumble the Original Oxo cube into 600 ml /1 pt boiling water. Pour the stock over the beef and add the passata, spices and oregano. Cover and cook for 1½ hours. Check the seasoning, adding salt and pepper if necessary.

5 Add the macaroni and cook for a further 40–45 minutes until the macaroni is tender. Stir after 30 minutes and add a little extra water if the casserole becomes too dry.

Cook ahead
Cook to the end of step 4. Re-heat the casserole, add the macaroni and continue to cook.

Chilli Beef Casserole

Quickly put together, this well-flavoured casserole of beef, vegetables and fruit, plus the subtle kick of chilli, needs no further attention while it simmers gently in the oven.

450 g / 1 lb thick cut top rump steak
30 ml / 2 tbsp seasoned flour
3 medium onions
1 green pepper
1 red pepper
5 ml / 1 tsp oil
450 g / 1 lb small new potatoes
2 Oxo Mexican Herb & Spice cubes
1 Original Oxo cube
45 ml / 3 tbsp tomato purée
30 ml / 2 tbsp red wine vinegar
411 g can peach halves in fruit juice

1 Cut the steak into four pieces and then coat with the seasoned flour. Peel and cut the onions into small wedges. Cut the peppers into quarters and remove the core and seeds.

2 Using a large non-stick frying pan, heat the oil, add the meat and cook quickly until well browned on both sides. Remove from the pan and put in a large casserole. Add the onions and peppers to the frying pan and cook until just golden brown, stirring occasionally. Add to the meat.

3 Add the potatoes to the casserole. In a bowl, mix together any remaining seasoned flour, the crumbled Mexican Herb & Spice and Original Oxo cubes, the tomato purée, vinegar and the juice from the can of peaches. Stir in 300 ml / ½ pt boiling water. Add the liquid to the casserole.

4 Cover and cook at 180°C/ 350°F/mark 4 for 1¼ hours or until the meat is tender.

5 Add the peaches, gently combining them with the meat and the vegetables. Cover and leave to stand for 2–3 minutes to heat the fruit.

Cook ahead

Prepare the casserole to the end of step 4, cool and refrigerate. Re-heat at 190°C/375°F/mark 5 for 30 minutes. Add the peaches and cook a further 10 minutes to heat the fruit.

OXO Tip
Use fresh peaches during the summer. To peel them, stand them in boiling water for about 30 seconds. Lift them out and gently remove the skins. You will need 3–4 peaches for this recipe.

Cook ahead, save time

Spring Lamb Casserole with Herb Dumplings

Cook the casserole in a large casserole dish so there is plenty of room for the dumplings to expand.

225 g / 8 oz small finger carrots
3 celery sticks
1 large leek
1 small onion
700 g / 1½ lb diced lamb
25 g / 1 oz butter
15 ml / 1 tbsp plain flour
1 Vegetable Oxo cube
300 ml / ½ pt dry cider
225 g / 8 oz green beans
Dumplings:
100 g / 4 oz self raising flour
1.25 ml / ¼ tsp baking powder
1 Oxo Italian Herb & Spice cube
40 g / 1½ oz shredded suet
15 ml / 1 tbsp chopped fresh parsley
salt and freshly ground pepper
100 ml / 4 fl oz milk

1 Scrub the carrots and trim the ends; cut the celery into 2.5 cm / 1 in pieces and thickly slice the leek, washing it well to remove any soil. Peel and slice the onion. Trim any excess fat from the lamb.

2 Heat the butter in a flameproof casserole, add the meat and cook for 4–5 minutes. Add the onion and cook for a further 3–5 minutes until golden. Stir in the flour.

3 Crumble the Vegetable cube into 450 ml / ¾ pt boiling water. Pour the stock into the casserole with the cider. Cover and bring to the boil. Then add the carrots, celery and leek. Cover and simmer for 1 hour.

4 Cut the green beans into 5 cm / 2 in lengths.

5 For the dumplings, sift the flour and baking powder into a bowl. Crumble in the Italian Herb & Spice cube. Add the suet and parsley, season and then add enough milk to form a soft dough (you may not need the full amount). Divide into 8 and shape into balls.

6 Stir the beans into the casserole, place the dumplings on top and simmer gently for 25 minutes.

Cook ahead
Prepare the casserole to the end of step 3, cool and refrigerate. Re-heat and add the beans and dumplings when it reaches simmering point.

Spiced Lamb Hotpot

I large onion
3 cloves garlic
30 ml / 2 tbsp oil
4 large chump ends of lamb
5 ml / I tsp ground ginger
10 ml / 2 tsp ground coriander
75 g / 3 oz green or brown lentils
2 Original Oxo cubes
30 ml / 2 tbsp Worcestershire sauce
salt and freshly ground pepper

1 Heat the oven to 170°C/ 325°F/mark 3. Peel and slice the onion and garlic. Heat the oil in a large flameproof casserole and brown the lamb. Set aside.

2 Add the onion to the pan. Cook for 4–5 minutes. Add the garlic and cook for 1 minute. Add the ginger, coriander and lentils.

3 Crumble the Original Oxo cubes into 900 ml / 1½ pt boiling water. Add to the casserole with the Worcestershire sauce.

4 Bring to the boil and replace the lamb. Cover and cook for 1 hour. Give the hotpot a stir and add a little water if necessary. Cook for a further 30 minutes. Season if necessary.

Cook ahead

Complete to the end of step 4. Cool and refrigerate. To re-heat, add a little water if necessary and heat in the oven at 190°C/375°F/mark 5 for about 30 minutes.

Cook ahead, save time

Chicken in Apricot Curry Sauce

1 small onion
5 ml / 1 tsp oil
100 ml / 4 fl oz red wine
15 ml / 1 tbsp tomato purée
30 ml / 2 tbsp lemon juice
2 Oxo Indian Herb & Spice cubes
411 g can apricot halves in fruit
  juice
150 ml / ¼ pt mayonnaise
150 ml / ¼ pt Greek yogurt
700 g / 1½ lb cold cooked chicken
lettuce, to garnish

1 Peel and chop the onion finely. Heat the oil in a non-stick saucepan and cook the onion until soft. Add the wine, tomato purée, lemon juice and crumbled Indian Herb & Spice cubes. Boil rapidly for about 5 minutes, stirring frequently, until reduced.

2 Drain the apricots. Roughly chop 6 apricot halves. Put the remaining apricots in a blender or food processor and process until smooth. (Or sieve them to make a purée.)

3 Mix together the apricot purée, mayonnaise, yogurt and cooled onion mixture.

4 Remove any skin from the chicken. Cut into bite-size pieces. Fold into the sauce with the chopped apricots. Serve garnished with lettuce leaves.

Cook ahead

Prepare the sauce to the end of step 3. Cover with cling film and refrigerate. Continue from step 4.

Turkey Cassoulet

Traditionally a cassoulet is made with belly pork, but turkey is a tasty, low-fat alternative. Serve this filling dish with a green salad. Freeze or microwave this dish without the topping. Add it at the end and crisp in the oven as described.

I Spanish onion
2 cloves garlic
I Chicken Oxo cube
45 ml / 3 tbsp olive oil
450 g / I lb diced turkey
100 g / 4 oz diced smoked bacon
225 g / 8 oz smoked pork sausage
397 g can chopped tomatoes
15 ml / I tbsp tomato purée
I Oxo Mexican Herb & Spice cube
400 g can borlotti beans
190 g baton of garlic bread

I Heat the oven to 180°C/ 350°F/mark 4. Peel and slice the onion. Peel and finely chop the garlic. Crumble the Chicken cube into 600 ml /1 pt boiling water.

2 Heat the oil in a large frying pan, add the turkey and bacon, and fry for about 5–6 minutes until golden. Transfer the meat to a large ovenproof casserole.

3 Put the onion in the frying pan and cook for 6–8 minutes until golden. Add the garlic and cook for 1 minute more. Add the onion and garlic to the casserole.

4 Thickly slice the pork sausage. Add it to the casserole with the stock, tomatoes and tomato purée. Crumble in the Mexican Herb & Spice cube and stir together. Cover the dish and cook for 45 minutes.

5 Meanwhile drain and rinse the beans. Cut the garlic bread into small pieces.

6 Stir the beans into the casserole. Scatter over the bread and return to the oven, uncovered, for 30 minutes until the bread is crisp and golden.

Cook ahead
Prepare to the end of stage 4. Stir in the beans and re-heat before adding the bread topping.

Golden Topped Pork and Butterbean Bake

This is an attractive-looking dish with a topping made from grated carrot and parsnip.

550 g / 1¼ lb boneless shoulder pork
1 medium onion
2 cloves garlic
3 celery sticks
30 ml / 2 tbsp oil
15 ml / 1 tbsp flour
2 Vegetable Oxo cubes
½ tsp dried thyme or 10 ml/ 2 tsp chopped fresh thyme
397 g can butterbeans
30 ml / 2 tbsp chopped fresh parsley
Topping:
350 g / 12 oz carrots
225 g / 8 oz parsnips or swede
25 g / 1 oz butter

1 Cut the pork into 4 cm / 1½ in cubes. Peel and chop the onion. Peel and crush the garlic. Slice the celery.

2 Heat the oil in a large saucepan, add the pork and cook for about 5 minutes until lightly browned. Remove and set aside.

3 Put the onion in the pan, and cook for 3–4 minutes until softened. Add the garlic and celery and cook for a further minute. Stir in the flour.

4 Crumble a Vegetable cube into 450 ml / ¾ pt boiling water. Pour the stock into the pan. Add the thyme and bring to a simmer. Cover the pan and cook gently for 1½ hours until the pork is tender.

5 Drain the butterbeans and stir into the casserole with the parsley.

6 Heat the oven to 180°C / 350°F / mark 4. Peel the carrots and parsnips or swede and coarsely grate. Melt the butter in a frying pan and add the vegetables. Crumble in the second Vegetable cube and stir-fry for 2–3 minutes.

7 Transfer the pork casserole to an ovenproof dish. Spoon over the grated vegetable mixture, and cook for 45 minutes.

Cook ahead

Cook the casserole to the end of stage 4. Cool and refrigerate. Resume cooking from stage 5 bringing the casserole up to the boil first.

Real Food for Kids

Sometimes it can be difficult coming up with new dishes to tempt kids' appetites – sometimes they surprise you and willingly eat exotic foods, yet reject plain foods. And, on top of all that, there's the worry of making sure they eat a proper, balanced diet. That's where Oxo can help by conjuring up some really super-tasting dishes (like the ones in this chapter) that will entice even the fussiest kids into sitting down and eating a proper, square meal.

Whatever your kids' tastes, try to make the food look attractive and colourful and dress up dishes with extra garnishes of vegetables. Make patterns with food for younger children and offer portions to suit their appetites, which can vary enormously.

'He put a snowball down my neck!'
'She started it!'

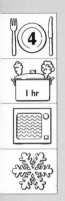

American-style Meatloaf with Tomato Sauce

This all-time favourite with children is served with a creamy tomato sauce. Accompany it with mashed potato and a green vegetable. You can, if you wish, microwave this recipe – you will need a loaf-shaped dish made from durable plastic, suitable for the microwave.

I small onion
I clove garlic
I egg
15 ml / I tbsp oil
450 g / I lb lean minced beef
50 g / 2 oz fresh breadcrumbs
2 Original Oxo cubes
3 tbsp chopped fresh parsley
15 ml / I tbsp tomato purée
Sauce:
I small onion
I small green pepper
15 ml / I tbsp olive oil
397 g can chopped tomatoes
I Oxo Italian Herb & Spice cube
60 ml / 4 tbsp double cream

1 Heat the oven to 180°C/ 350°F/mark 4. Peel and chop the onion. Peel and crush the garlic. Beat the egg lightly.

2 Heat the oil in a small pan, add the onion and cook gently until the onion is soft. Add the garlic and cook for 1 minute more.

3 Turn the onion and garlic into a large bowl. Add the minced beef and breadcrumbs. Crumble the 2 Original Oxo cubes into 75 ml / 3 fl oz boiling water. Then add the stock to the bowl with the parsley, egg and tomato purée. Mix well.

4 Turn the mixture into a lightly oiled 450 g / 1 lb loaf tin. Bake for 1 hour. Allow the loaf to stand for 10 minutes before turning it out.

5 Meanwhile make the sauce. Peel the onion and chop very finely. Remove the core and seeds from the pepper and chop it finely (this may be easier in a food processor).

6 Heat the oil in a small saucepan. Add the onion and pepper and cook for 3–4 minutes. Add the chopped tomatoes and crumble in the Italian Herb & Spice cube. Simmer for 15 minutes until thick and pulpy. Stir in the cream and simmer for 3–4 minutes.

7 Serve the meatloaf in slices with the sauce.

Lentil and Carrot Burgers

For young children, you can form the mixture into smaller size burgers; for teenagers make them slightly larger and serve them in bread buns with their favourite sauces. If there is only one vegetarian in the family, make up a batch of burgers and freeze them on a tray at the end of step 4. Pack in polythene bags and keep them for up to 6 months. You can thaw as many as are required and cook them under the grill as described in step 5. Serve them with a green or mixed salad.

175 g / 6 oz red lentils
1 Vegetable Oxo cube
1 small onion
225 g / 8 oz carrots
30 ml / 2 tbsp olive oil
50 g / 2 oz fresh breadcrumbs
25 g / 1 oz porridge oats
1 Oxo Italian Herb & Spice cube
30 ml / 2 tbsp chopped fresh parsley

1 Put the lentils in a saucepan. Crumble the Vegetable cube into 450 ml / ¾ pt hot water. Pour the stock over the lentils and simmer for 15 minutes, until the lentils are tender and most of the stock has been absorbed.

2 Meanwhile, peel the onion and carrots, and chop them finely. Heat the oil in a frying pan, add the vegetables and cook for 3–4 minutes. Turn the onions and carrots into a bowl.

3 Drain any excess water from the lentils and add them to the bowl. Then add the breadcrumbs, oats, crumbled Italian Herb & Spice cube and the parsley. Mix well.

4 Form the mixture into 8 'patty' shapes.

5 Heat the grill. Put the burgers on a greased baking tray, brush them with oil and cook for about 4–5 minutes on each side until golden.

OXO Tip
Take care as you pat the burgers into shape and don't handle them more than you need to. It is easier to shape the mixture with wet hands. Use a fish slice to put them on the baking tray.

Cheese Burgers

Do not be tempted to put the burgers too close to the grill – they will burn and dry out if cooked too fast.

700 g / 1½ lb extra lean minced beef
2 Original Oxo cubes
freshly ground pepper
1 small onion
1 egg, size 3 or 4
15 ml / 1 tsp tomato purée
100 g / 4 oz mature Cheddar cheese
4 rashers streaky bacon
4 soft hamburger rolls
crisp lettuce leaves

1 Break the beef into small pieces. Crumble over the Original Oxo cubes and season with pepper. Peel and chop the onion finely and add to the beef. Break the egg into a small bowl and lightly mix in the tomato purée. Add to the beef and thoroughly blend. Divide and shape into burgers. Cut half of the cheese into 4 cubes. Press a cube into the centre of each burger, shaping the mixture around to enclose it completely. Wrap a bacon rasher around each burger, securing it with a cocktail stick.

2 Grill the burgers for 6–8 minutes each side.

3 Grate the remaining cheese. Sprinkle over the burgers.

4 Split the rolls. Put 1 or 2 lettuce leaves in each. Add the burgers. Serve immediately.

Honey Glazed Ribs

Children love to pick up food to eat – give them plenty of kitchen paper to wipe sticky fingers.

45 mins

3 Oxo Chinese Herb & Spice cubes
60 ml / 4 tbsp orange juice
60 ml / 4 tbsp tomato ketchup
30 ml / 2 tbsp clear honey
15 ml / I tbsp wine vinegar
900 g / 2 lb American-style pork ribs

1 Crumble the Chinese Herb & Spice cubes into the orange juice. Stir in the tomato ketchup, honey and vinegar.

2 Put the ribs in a large ovenproof dish. Pour over the marinade and make sure the ribs are thoroughly coated. Cover and refrigerate for at least 1 hour or leave overnight.

3 Heat the oven to 190°C / 375°F / mark 5. Cook the ribs for 45 minutes to 1 hour until tender and brown, turning them every 15 minutes and basting with the marinade to keep them moist.

Crisp Chicken Nuggets with two Sauces

For an informal meal, serve the Chicken Nuggets in a basket with potato crisps and a simple salad, such as cherry tomatoes and sticks of cucumber.

2 garlic cloves
I Chicken Oxo cube
150 ml / ¼ pt natural yogurt
I lemon
30 ml / 2 tbsp tomato purée
freshly ground pepper
4 skinned boneless chicken breasts
I Vegetable Oxo cube
75 g / 3 oz fresh breadcrumbs
Barbecue sauce:
I small onion
10 ml / 2 tsp oil
150 ml / ¼ pt tomato ketchup
30 ml / 2 tbsp demerara sugar
15 ml / I tbsp vinegar
15 ml / I tbsp Worcestershire sauce
5 ml / I tsp Dijon mustard
Mint dip:
30 ml / 2 tbsp mint jelly
150 ml / ¼ pt natural yogurt
freshly ground pepper

I Peel and crush the garlic. Crumble the Chicken cube into the yogurt and add the garlic. Grate the lemon rind and squeeze the juice. Add to the yogurt with the tomato purée. Season with pepper.

2 Cut each chicken breast into 4 cubes and put them in a glass dish. Whisk the yogurt marinade and pour it over the chicken. Mix everything together so that the chicken is well coated. Cover and refrigerate for 2–3 hours or overnight.

3 On a sheet of greaseproof paper, mix together the crumbled Vegetable cube and breadcrumbs. Using a fork, lift each piece of chicken on to the crumbs and turn it to coat all the sides. Put the pieces on a lightly oiled baking tray. Bake at 180°C/350°F/mark 4 for 20–25 minutes or until golden.

4 Meanwhile, make the sauces. For the barbecue sauce, peel and chop the onion finely. Heat the oil in a small pan, add the onion and cook until soft. Add the remaining ingredients and simmer for 5 minutes.

5 For the mint dip, whisk the mint jelly into the yogurt and season with pepper. Serve the chicken hot with the sauces.

OXO Tip
Provide plenty of serviettes or kitchen towel!

4

25 mins

Spicy Frankfurter and Potato Hash

A quick and easy meal to prepare for lunch or supper.

1 medium onion
350 g / 12 oz potatoes
45 ml / 3 tbsp sunflower oil
1 Original Oxo cube
1 Oxo Mexican Herb & Spice cube
8 skinless frankfurters
420 g can baked beans

1 Peel and chop the onion. Dice the potatoes.

2 Heat the oil in a large frying pan. Add the onions and potatoes and cook until the potatoes are browned, stirring them around while cooking – this should take 8–10 minutes.

3 Crumble the Original Oxo cube into 300 ml / ½ pt boiling water. Pour the stock into the pan and add the Mexican Herb & Spice cube. Boil until the potatoes are tender. During this time, most of the liquid will evaporate.

4 Cut the frankfurters into 2.5 cm / 1 in pieces. Add them to the pan with the baked beans and cook gently together for 5 minutes.

Rainbow Pasta

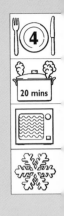

40 g / 1½ oz butter
75 g / 3 oz fresh white breadcrumbs
2 Oxo Italian Herb & Spice cubes
175 g / 6 oz pasta bows
15 ml / 1 tbsp oil
175 g / 6 oz lightly smoked diced
  bacon
397 g can chopped tomatoes
198 g can sweetcorn kernels
50 g / 2 oz frozen peas
30 ml / 2 tbsp chopped fresh parsley

1 Melt the butter in a frying pan, add the breadcrumbs and fry for about 5 minutes until crisp and golden. Spoon them out onto a double thickness of kitchen paper and set aside.

2 Crumble an Italian Herb & Spice cube into a pan of boiling salted water, add the pasta and cook until just tender – about 8 minutes. Drain well.

3 Meanwhile, wipe out the frying pan with kitchen paper and add the oil. Fry the bacon for 3 minutes until golden. Pour in the tomatoes and add the second Italian Herb & Spice cube. Simmer for 5 minutes until thick and pulpy.

4 Add the sweetcorn and peas to the frying pan and stir. Simmer for 5 minutes. Add the pasta and heat through.

5 Spoon the pasta into a serving dish. Sprinkle with the breadcrumbs and chopped parsley.

4

25 mins

Deep-Pan Pizza

This recipe uses a scone mixture instead of bread dough for the base. For a Mexican flavour, you can substitute cornmeal for half the flour and add 2.5 ml / ½ tsp baking powder. Vary the toppings. Instead of pepperoni, you could use grilled sliced sausages, or mushrooms if you are cooking for vegetarians. Add other vegetables that children like, such as sweetcorn, broccoli (blanch it first) or courgettes. Look out for special grated pizza cheese in supermarkets – usually a combination of Cheddar and Mozzarella.

150 ml / ¼ pt passata
30 ml / 2 tbsp tomato purée
2 Oxo Italian Herb & Spice cubes
Base:
350 g / 12 oz self-raising flour
75 g / 3 oz margarine
200 ml / 7 fl oz milk
Topping:
3 tomatoes
1 green pepper
75 g / 3 oz sliced pepperoni, diced ham, or diced cooked chicken
75 g / 3 oz grated Cheddar or Mozzarella cheese

1 Heat the oven to 220°C/ 425°F/mark 7. Put the passata into a small saucepan with the tomato purée. Crumble in 1 Italian Herb & Spice cube and simmer until well blended. Set aside.

2 Sift the flour into a bowl. Crumble in the second Italian Herb & Spice cube, add the margarine and rub together until blended. Add the milk and mix to make a soft dough.

3 Knead lightly, and then roll out into a round (25.5 cm/ 10 in diameter). Transfer the round to a greased baking tray, and bake it for 10 minutes until golden and risen.

4 Meanwhile, slice the tomatoes. Remove the core and seeds from the pepper and slice it thinly.

5 Remove the pizza base from the oven. Spread the tomato sauce over it, and then arrange the tomatoes, pepperoni and green pepper on top and scatter over the cheese.

6 Return to the oven at 200°C/ 400°F/mark 6 and cook for 10–12 minutes until the base is cooked and the top is bubbling. Cool a little before serving.

Real Food for Kids

74

HEALTHY AND LIGHT

Most people embark on some sort of diet at least once in their lives. Whether you're counting calories or simply on the look-out for healthy dishes that don't compromise on taste, these recipes embrace many of the current recommendations on healthy eating. Most are very quick to prepare and so if you're rushing off to a sports centre – or an exercise class is on the agenda – these would be ideal recipes to have in your culinary repertoire.

'I haven't used a pair of these since we were in the Orient.'

Provençal Chicken with Lemon and Parsley Garnish

This dish, of chicken breasts in a tomato-based sauce, is topped with a garnish of lemon rind, garlic and parsley – called 'persillade' in France. If you are cooking the chicken in a microwave, use a browning dish. Serve with rice or jacket potatoes.

1 large lemon
1 Chicken Oxo cube
1 garlic clove
30 ml / 2 tbsp chopped fresh parsley
1 medium onion
2 peppers, yellow, red or green
15 ml / 1 tbsp olive oil
4 boneless, skinless chicken breasts
400 g can chopped tomatoes
2 Oxo Italian Herb & Spice cubes
12 stoned black olives
freshly ground pepper

1 Grate the lemon rind and put in a small bowl. Squeeze the juice from the lemon and pour it into a measuring jug. Crumble in the Chicken cube and add boiling water to make 150 ml / ¼ pt liquid.

2 Peel the garlic and chop it finely. Mix together the lemon rind, garlic and parsley. Set aside.

3 Peel and slice the onion thinly. Remove the core and seeds from the pepper. Cut it into thick slices.

4 Heat the oil in a large non-stick frying pan and add the onion. Cook the onion until soft and then add the chicken. Cook until golden brown on both sides.

5 Add the stock to the pan with the peppers and chopped tomatoes. Crumble in the Italian Herb & Spice cubes. Simmer uncovered for 30 minutes until the chicken and peppers are tender.

6 Add the olives and season if necessary. Serve sprinkled with the lemon persillade.

OXO Tip
Do not freeze the grated lemon rind garnish. Make it fresh and add just before serving to give the dish a delicious citrus aroma.

Chicken and Tarragon Soup

1 small onion
2 medium carrots
2 chicken thighs
15 g / ½ oz butter
2 Chicken Oxo cubes
150 ml / ¼ pt white wine
30 ml / 2 tbsp chopped fresh
   tarragon
10 ml / 2 tsp flour
450 ml / ¾ pt semi-skimmed milk

1 Peel and finely chop the onion. Peel and dice the carrots. Remove the skin from the chicken and then take out the bones. Discard the skin and bones.

2 Melt the butter in a non-stick saucepan. Add the onion and cook for 5 minutes until soft, stirring frequently.

3 Add the chicken and cook, stirring until lightly browned. Stir in the carrots.

4 Crumble the Chicken cubes into 450 ml /¾ pt boiling water and stir in the wine and tarragon. Pour over the chicken.

5 Bring to the boil, then cover and simmer gently for about 20 minutes until the chicken is tender.

6 Lift out the chicken and finely chop it.

7 Purée half the soup in a blender or food processor. Add the flour and blend again. Return the purée to the saucepan and add the chicken.

8 Stir in the milk and heat to serving temperature, stirring continuously, but do not boil.

OXO Tip

This soup is ideal for using up cooked chicken (perhaps from a whole roast bird). At step 5 simmer the chicken for 5 minutes until it is heated through and flavoured with the stock.

Mexican Chicken with Fresh Tomato Salsa

Don't be tempted to skip the marinating if you want the flavour to be authentic. Serve with the chilled spicy tomato sauce, rice and, for those not watching their weight, some soured cream and Mexican corn chips.

2 Oxo Mexican Herb & Spice cubes
30 ml / 2 tbsp tomato ketchup
30 ml / 2 tbsp + 5 ml / I tsp oil
4 skinned boneless chicken breasts
I medium onion
450 g / I lb ripe tomatoes
finely grated rind of I lemon
15 ml / I tbsp lemon juice
fresh coriander, to garnish

1 Whisk 1 crumbled Mexican Herb & Spice cube with the tomato ketchup and 30 ml / 2 tbsp oil. Pour into a shallow dish and add the chicken, turning it to coat both sides. Cover and leave in the refrigerator to marinate for 30 minutes or more.

2 For the salsa, peel and finely chop the onion. Put the tomatoes in a bowl, pour over boiling water, leave for a few seconds, and then drain and plunge into cold water. Peel off the skin and finely chop the flesh, discarding the seeds if preferred.

3 Heat the remaining oil in a non-stick frying pan and stir in the onion and remaining crumbled Mexican Herb & Spice cube. Cook over medium heat, stirring constantly, until just soft but not browned. Tip into a bowl.

4 Stir in the lemon rind and juice and the tomatoes. Stir well, cover and chill the salsa until required.

5 Grill or barbecue the chicken for 20–25 minutes until cooked through. Garnish with coriander and serve with the tomato salsa.

OXO Tip
Great for a barbecue. Any small portions of chicken such as drumsticks or thighs are suitable for cooking this way, but remember that chicken thigh meat needs slightly longer cooking than breast meat.

Healthy and Light

82

Tandoori Chicken

If time allows, marinating the chicken for 1–2 hours enhances the tandoori flavour. Add a few drops of orange or red food colouring to the yogurt marinade if you like.

4 chicken drumsticks
4 chicken thighs
1 garlic clove
2 Oxo Indian Herb & Spice cubes
150 ml / ¼ pt natural set yogurt
5 ml / 1 tsp red wine vinegar
15 ml / 1 tbsp tomato purée

1 Remove the skin from the chicken pieces and then make three or four cuts in the thickest side of each piece.

2 Peel and crush the garlic. Crumble the Indian Herb & Spice cubes into the yogurt and stir in the garlic, vinegar and tomato purée. Spread the mixture thickly over all sides of the chicken pieces. Cover and leave in the refrigerator to marinate for at least 30 minutes.

3 Arrange the chicken on a wire rack, standing on a baking tray, and spoon any marinade over the chicken. Cook at 190°C / 375°F / mark 5 for 20–30 minutes until the chicken is golden brown and cooked through.

Indian Plaice and Spinach Rolls

1 small onion
225 g / 8 oz fresh spinach or 100 g /
    4 oz frozen leaf spinach, thawed
    and thoroughly drained
10 ml / 2 tsp oil
2 Oxo Indian Herb & Spice cubes
50 g / 2 oz low-fat cream cheese
8 medium skinless plaice fillets
25 g / 1 oz butter
50 g / 2 oz fresh white breadcrumbs

1 Peel and slice the onion thinly. Wash the fresh spinach. Tear into small pieces.

2 Preheat the oven to 190°C / 375°F / mark 5.

3 Heat the oil in a saucepan, add the onion and cook until golden and soft. Crumble in 1 Indian Herb & Spice cube. Add the spinach. Cook, stirring, until the spinach, if fresh, has wilted, and all the water has evaporated.

4 Remove the pan from the heat. Stir in the cream cheese.

5 Place a spoonful of the mixture at the narrow end of each fillet – on the skin side – and roll up. Arrange the rolls in a greased ovenproof dish.

6 In a small saucepan melt the butter, stir in the breadcrumbs and crumble in 1 Indian Herb & Spice cube. Mix together. Spoon the mixture over the plaice rolls, pressing down lightly.

7 Bake the rolls for 20 minutes until the topping is golden.

Summer Tortilla

This is delicious made with Jersey Royal potatoes, but any new potatoes will do. Serve it with a green salad and – for those not counting calories – crusty bread.

225 g / 8 oz new potatoes
100 g / 4 oz onion
1 clove garlic
1 red pepper
1 green pepper
225 g / 8 oz tomatoes
6 eggs
2 Oxo Italian Herb & Spice cubes
salt and freshly ground pepper
30 ml / 2 tbsp olive oil

1 Boil the potatoes in salted water for about 20 minutes, until tender. Drain them and cut into 2.5 cm / 1 in chunks.

2 Peel and slice the onion. Peel and crush the garlic. Remove the core and seeds from the peppers and slice them. Skin the tomatoes and roughly chop.

3 Break the eggs into a bowl. Crumble in the Italian Herb & Spice cubes, add a little salt and pepper and beat together.

4 Heat the oil in a medium-size frying pan. Add the onion and cook it until golden. Stir in the garlic, peppers and potatoes and cook for 3–4 minutes.

5 Add the tomatoes to the pan. Pour over the eggs and cook over a low heat for about 8–10 minutes until the egg is almost set. Place the pan under a hot grill to finish cooking the top of the tortilla.

6 Serve the tortilla cut into wedges, either hot or cold.

OXO Tip

In Spain tortilla is very often eaten cold. It makes an ideal picnic dish or packed lunch.

Oriental Beef Salad

The marinade and juices from the beef make a low-calorie dressing for this salad.

3 Oxo Chinese Herb & Spice cubes
30 ml / 2 tbsp tomato purée
450 g / I lb very lean rump steak
225 g / 8 oz broccoli
225 g / 8 oz pack of baby sweetcorn
  and mangetout
I red pepper
30 ml / 2 tbsp sunflower oil
15 ml / I tbsp sesame seeds

1 Crumble the Chinese Herb & Spice cubes into a dish. Add the tomato purée and 30 ml / 2 tbsp water and mix together. Cut the beef into thin strips and add to the marinade. Mix well and then set aside for 30 minutes to 1 hour.

2 Meanwhile, thinly slice the stalks from the broccoli and divide it into small florets. Cut the sweetcorn into thick slices and trim and halve the mangetout. Remove the core and seeds from the pepper and cut it into thin strips.

3 Heat a large pan of water. Add the broccoli and sweetcorn and simmer for 2 minutes. Add the mangetout and simmer for a further minute. Drain the vegetables and turn them into a serving dish. Allow them to cool and then add the red pepper strips.

4 Heat the oil in a large non-stick frying pan, add the beef and cook over a high heat for 4–5 minutes, stirring all the time. Cool a little and then tip the beef into the vegetables with the juices from the pan and toss together. Cover and refrigerate.

5 To serve, scatter over the sesame seeds.

OXO Tip
Many supermarkets now sell packs of mixed baby sweetcorn and mangetout. If these are not available, then either buy sweetcorn and mangetout separately or substitute raw mushrooms, raw spring onions or a small can of sweetcorn kernels.

Turkish Meatballs with Minted Yogurt

You could cook these meatballs on a barbecue – or, if you prefer, under the grill. Thread them on metal skewers so you can turn them easily. They are very tasty served with warmed pitta bread (this will add approximately 80 calories to your meal). The meatballs will freeze quite easily, but make the sauce just before you need it.

I small onion
I clove garlic
450 g / I lb extra lean minced beef
I Original Oxo cube
5 ml / I tsp dried oregano
2.5 ml / ½ tsp ground allspice
150 ml / ¼ pt low-fat natural yogurt
5 ml / I tsp mint sauce
shredded lettuce, to serve

1 Peel and finely chop the onion. Peel and crush the garlic and put the onion and garlic in a bowl with the minced beef. Crumble over the Original Oxo cube and add the oregano, allspice and 30 ml / 2 tbsp of the yogurt.

2 Using your fingers, knead the ingredients together until the mixture sticks together and looks paste-like. Divide into 16 portions. Heat the grill.

3 With wet hands, shape the portions into ovals. Place on a grill rack.

4 Cook under the grill for about 10 minutes, turning the meatballs with tongs, until browned all over.

5 Meanwhile, mix the mint sauce into the rest of the yogurt.

6 Serve immediately with shredded lettuce and minted yogurt.

OXO Tip
Extra lean minced beef is now easily available in supermarkets. With only 5–8% fat, it is a great help in reducing the amount of fat in the diet.

VEGETARIAN DELIGHTS

Vegetarian eating is becoming more and more popular and the age group most affected is teenagers. At this age it is very important that a wide range of foods are eaten to provide all the necessary nutrients for growth and development. Try to make dishes with lots of different vegetables and pulses and use the recipes in this chapter to introduce your vegetarian family and friends to new ideas and tastes. You'll find these dishes are so delicious that there is no reason why everyone – vegetarian or non-vegetarian – shouldn't enjoy them.

'How's your pulse, Alison?'

Courgette Risotto

Risottos are traditionally very moist and are served in shallow bowls with a spoon and fork. In this recipe the courgettes steam on top of the rice so that they retain their beautiful colour and are still slightly crisp to the bite

1 medium onion
225 g / 8 oz small courgettes
25 g / 1 oz pine kernels
30 ml / 2 tbsp olive oil
1 Vegetable Oxo cube
1 Oxo Italian Herb & Spice cube
50 ml / 2 fl oz dry white vermouth
  or wine
100 g / 4 oz arborio (risotto) rice
freshly ground pepper
25 g / 1 oz shaved or freshly grated
  Parmesan cheese

1 Peel and slice the onion thinly. Slice the courgettes thickly.

2 Put the pine kernels in a small, dry non-stick pan and cook over a high heat until golden. Set the kernels aside.

3 Heat the oil in a saucepan, add the onion and cook over a medium heat until soft and golden.

4 Crumble the Vegetable cube into 450 ml / ¾ pt boiling water. Crumble in the Italian Herb & Spice cube and stir in the vermouth or wine.

5 Add the rice to the onion and cook, stirring, for 2–3 minutes. Stir in about a quarter of the hot stock, and allow the stock to simmer until it has been absorbed by the rice.

6 Pour another quarter of stock into the pan and simmer again until it has been absorbed. Add the rest of the stock, place the courgettes on top of the rice, and then cover and simmer for 20 minutes until the rice is tender.

7 Stir the courgettes into the rice with the Parmesan cheese. Season if necessary and serve the risotto with the pine kernels scattered on top.

OXO Tip
For an even quicker dish you can use the microwave. Cook the onion for 3 minutes. Add the rice and cook for a minute more. Add the stock and cook for another 5 minutes. Finally add the courgettes and cook for 5–7 minutes or until the rice is tender.

Vegetarian Delights

Aubergine Parmigiana

Salting the sliced aubergine removes excess moisture and any bitterness.

900 g / 2 lb aubergines
salt
1 medium onion
1 garlic clove
400 g can chopped tomatoes
50 ml / 2 fl oz dry white vermouth
10 ml / 2 tsp sugar
2 Oxo Italian Herb & Spice cubes
60 ml / 4 tbsp olive oil
225 g / 8 oz Mozzarella cheese
45 ml / 3 tbsp freshly grated
Parmesan cheese

1 Slice the aubergines into 1 cm / ½ in slices. Put the slices in a colander, sprinkling each layer generously with salt. Leave to drain for 30 minutes.

2 Meanwhile, peel and thinly slice the onion. Peel and crush the garlic. Put the onion, garlic, tomatoes, vermouth and sugar in a medium saucepan. Crumble in the Italian Herb & Spice cubes and stir together. Bring just to the boil. Reduce the heat to medium-low and cook for 20 minutes until the onion is just soft.

3 Rinse the aubergine slices and pat dry with kitchen paper. Arrange in a single layer on an oiled baking tray. Brush lightly with olive oil. Grill until golden brown, turning over once.

4 Grate the Mozzarella cheese. Arrange one third of the aubergine slices in a shallow baking dish. Spoon over half the tomato sauce and sprinkle with one third of the Mozzarella cheese. Add a second layer of aubergine, the remaining sauce and one third of the Mozzarella cheese. Add a final layer of aubergine and top with the remaining Mozzarella cheese. Sprinkle the Parmesan cheese on top.

5 Bake at 200°C / 400°F / mark 6 for 20 minutes until golden brown. Leave to stand for 10 minutes before serving.

OXO *Tip*
To make doubly sure that your aubergine dish will not be bitter, always choose the firmest, shiniest aubergines and use them while they are still absolutely fresh.

Tofu with Sweet Pepper Sauce

Tofu (soy bean curd) is sold in several different forms and this recipe uses the firm plain version, available in supermarkets and health food shops. Low in fat, tofu is a good source of protein and should therefore be included on both vegetarian and non-vegetarian menus.

2 × 220 g packets plain tofu
I large onion
I garlic clove
2 large red peppers
30 ml / 2 tbsp plain flour
2 Oxo Italian Herb & Spice cubes
15 ml / I tbsp oil
I Vegetable Oxo cube
225 g / 8 oz pasta

1 Drain the tofu and cut into 2.5 cm / 1 in cubes. Peel and thinly slice the onion. Peel and crush the garlic. Cut the peppers in half, discard the core and seeds and dice the flesh.

2 Combine the flour and crumbled Italian Herb & Spice cubes on a sheet of greaseproof paper. Add the tofu and coat on all sides with the seasoned flour.

3 Heat the oil in a large non-stick frying pan and add the tofu. Cook over high heat, turning frequently, until golden brown on all sides. Remove from the pan with a slotted spoon.

4 Add the onion and garlic to the pan. Cook over medium-high heat until soft and beginning to brown. Add the peppers and cook for a further 2–3 minutes.

5 Crumble over the Vegetable cube and add 300 ml / ½ pt boiling water. Stir well. Return the tofu to the pan. Cover and cook over medium heat for 10 minutes.

6 Meanwhile, cook the pasta following the packet instructions.

7 Drain the pasta and serve, topped with the tofu and pepper sauce.

Vegetarian Delights

OXO Tip
Try this recipe using smoked tofu.

15 mins

Ravioli Parmesan

Choose any filled pasta for this recipe, either fresh or dried.
Grated Cheddar can be used in place of Parmesan cheese. Serve
with a salad of avocado wedges and chicory.

I small onion
I garlic clove
230 g can chopped tomatoes
10 ml / 2 tsp tomato purée
10 ml / 2 tsp sugar
5 ml / I tsp red wine vinegar
I Oxo Italian Herb & Spice cube
freshly ground pepper
225 g / 8 oz fresh or dried filled
   pasta
25 g / I oz freshly grated Parmesan
   cheese

1 Peel and finely chop the onion. Peel and crush the garlic.

2 Put the onion, garlic, tomatoes, tomato purée, sugar and vinegar in a small saucepan.

3 Crumble over the Italian Herb & Spice cube and stir to combine. Season with pepper.

4 Bring just to the boil, cover and reduce the heat to medium-low. Simmer for 10 minutes.

5 Meanwhile, cook the pasta in a large saucepan or frying pan of barely simmering water. Cook gently until just tender. Drain well and place in a shallow flameproof dish.

6 Spoon over the sauce and lightly mix together. Sprinkle over the Parmesan cheese and grill until golden brown.

OXO *Tip*
Filled pasta often cooks more successfully in a single layer in a
frying pan. Simmer gently to prevent the pasta breaking open.

10 mins

Vegetable Chow Mein

175 g / 6 oz medium egg noodles
10 cm / 4 in piece of cucumber
227 g can water chestnuts, drained
100 g / 4 oz small spinach leaves or Chinese leaves
2 Oxo Chinese Herb & Spice cubes
15 ml / 1 tbsp dry sherry
30 ml / 2 tbsp soy sauce
5 ml / 1 tsp sugar
5 ml / 1 tsp cornflour
5 ml / 1 tsp + 15 ml / 1 tbsp oil
75 g / 3 oz roasted unsalted cashew nuts
100 g / 4 oz bean sprouts

1 Cook the noodles following packet instructions.

2 Cut the cucumber into 2.5 cm /1 in slices, halve them lengthways, remove the seeds and cut into matchsticks. Halve the water chestnuts horizontally. Slice the spinach or Chinese leaves.

3 To make the glaze, crumble the Chinese Herb & Spice cubes into a bowl and stir in the sherry, soy sauce, sugar and cornflour.

4 Heat the 5 ml /1 tsp oil in a non-stick wok or large frying pan. Add the cashew nuts and cook until golden brown, stirring constantly. Remove from the pan.

5 Drain the noodles thoroughly. Heat the remaining oil in the wok, add the noodles and cook over a high heat for 3 minutes, stirring constantly.

6 Add the cucumber, chestnuts and bean sprouts and cook for 2 minutes, stirring constantly.

7 Add the glaze and cook for 30 seconds, stirring to coat the noodles and vegetables. Stir in the spinach or Chinese leaves. Serve immediately, topped with the nuts.

OXO Tip
Other colourful ingredients can be added to this recipe or substituted for existing ingredients – peppers, mangetout, spring onions. To reduce the calorie count leave out the nuts and add some mushrooms.

Vegetarian Delights

Vegetable Curry

This is a medium-hot curry. Don't be tempted to fry garlic over a high heat – if it becomes too brown it will taste bitter.

1 large onion
1 garlic clove
225 g / 8 oz carrots
100 g / 4 oz button mushrooms
15 ml / 1 tbsp oil
3 Oxo Indian Herb & Spice cubes
225 g / 8 oz small cauliflower florets
225 g / 8 oz green beans
40 g / 1½ oz creamed coconut

1 Peel and thinly slice the onion. Peel and crush the garlic. Peel and thickly slice the carrots. Wash and dry the mushrooms and cut any large ones in half.

2 Heat the oil in a non-stick saucepan and cook the onion and garlic until soft, stirring frequently.

3 Crumble the Indian Herb & Spice cubes over the onion and cook for 1–2 minutes, stirring.

4 Add all the remaining vegetables and 300 ml / ½ pt water.

5 Bring to the boil, cover and simmer gently for about 15 minutes or until the vegetables are just tender, gently stirring occasionally.

6 Meanwhile, finely chop the coconut. When the vegetables are tender, add to the pan and gently stir until it dissolves. Serve hot.

Vegetarian Delights

White Bean and Mushroom Soup

2 Vegetable Oxo cubes
2 x 432 g can cannellini beans
2 garlic cloves
25 g / 1 oz butter
125 g / 4 oz baby button
  mushrooms
150 ml / ¼ pt single cream
30 ml / 2 tbsp dry sherry
salt and freshly ground pepper
30 ml / 2 tbsp snipped chives, to
  garnish

1 Crumble the Vegetable cubes into 600 ml / 1 pt boiling water. Drain the beans and rinse under cold running water. Peel and crush the garlic.

2 Put the beans into a food processor or blender with half the stock and process until smooth.

3 Melt the butter in a large saucepan, add the mushrooms and cook over a high heat, until golden. Remove and set aside. Add the garlic to the pan and cook for a minute. Do not allow the garlic to brown.

4 Add the bean purée to the pan with the rest of the stock and the cream. Simmer for 5 minutes.

5 Stir in the sherry and season if necessary. Garnish with the mushrooms and chives.

Vegetarian Delights

105

10 mins

Creamy Beans with Parmesan Toasts

1 medium onion
3 celery sticks
1 garlic clove
213 g can butter or cannellini beans
213 g can kidney beans
75 ml / 3 fl oz single cream
75 ml / 3 fl oz natural yogurt
5 ml / 1 tsp cornflour
2 Vegetable Oxo cubes
freshly ground pepper
5 ml / 1 tsp + 15 ml / 1 tbsp oil
2 thick slices of bread
30 ml / 2 tbsp freshly grated
   Parmesan cheese

1 Peel and thinly slice the onion. Separate into rings. Very thinly slice the celery. Peel and crush the garlic. Drain and rinse the beans under cold running water, then drain well.

2 Whisk together the cream, yogurt, cornflour, 1 Vegetable cube and season with pepper.

3 Heat 5 ml / 1 tsp of the oil in a non-stick frying pan and add the onion, celery and garlic. Cook over medium-high heat, stirring frequently, until soft and beginning to brown. Stir in the beans.

4 Add the cream mixture and heat, stirring frequently, until bubbling hot.

5 Crumble the second Vegetable cube into the remaining oil and stir to combine. Spoon over one side of each of the slices of bread and sprinkle with the cheese. Grill until golden brown.

6 Serve the Creamy Beans spooned on to the hot toasts.

OXO Tip
Vary this dish by adding a small pepper. Roughly chop the flesh and add with the other vegetables to the frying pan.

4

I hr 5 mins

Moroccan Vegetable Couscous

Look out for couscous in supermarkets. It is similar to semolina and is easy to prepare either by soaking or steaming. By all means freeze the vegetable sauce, but prepare the couscous just before you need it.

225 g / 8 oz carrots
450 g / I lb turnips, swede or
    celeriac
I large onion
2 cloves garlic
30 ml / 2 tbsp olive oil
5 ml / I tsp ground cumin
5 ml / I tsp ground coriander
2.5 ml / ½ tsp paprika
2.5 ml / ½ tsp turmeric
15 ml / I tbsp tomato purée
2 Vegetable Oxo cubes
225 g / 8 oz couscous
2 medium courgettes
50 g / 2 oz raisins
400 g can chickpeas
40 g / 1½ oz butter
15 ml / I tbsp chopped parsley
15 ml / I tbsp chopped coriander

I Peel and thickly slice the carrots. Peel and dice the turnips, swede or celeriac. Peel and slice the onion and peel and finely chop the garlic.

2 Heat the oil in a large saucepan. Add the vegetables and cook for about 5 minutes, stirring until they become golden.

3 Stir in all the spices and then add the tomato purée. Crumble one of the Vegetable cubes into 600 ml / 1 pt boiling water, and then pour into the pan. Cover and simmer for 30 minutes.

4 Put the couscous into a bowl. Crumble the second Vegetable cube into 600 ml / 1 pt hot water. Pour the stock over the couscous and allow it to stand for 30 minutes until all the liquid is absorbed.

5 Slice the courgettes, add to the pan with the raisins and drained chickpeas. Continue to simmer for 30 minutes.

6 Melt the butter in a large frying pan, add the couscous and stir it around until it is heated through and the grains are separated.

7 Stir the chopped herbs into the vegetables and then serve them with the couscous.

Vegetarian Delights

EASY GOURMET FOOD

Most of us, when cooking a special meal for friends or family, like to experiment with unusual ingredients or try a new recipe. It's a welcome opportunity to lavish a little more time, care and attention than we generally have available for everyday meals. But however much we'd like to shine, cooking a new dish can be a hair-raising experience. Here at Oxo we know that the most successful meals are the ones that you enjoy cooking just as much as your guests enjoy eating them and so all the recipes in this chapter have been created to be simple, straightforward, no-risk Oxo classics from the very first time you try them out.

'This is nice, Nick. Just the two of us then?'

15 mins

Seafood Primavera

Serve this dish of colourful vegetables and fish in shallow bowls to eat with a fork and spoon. Accompany it with toasted crusty bread.

½ yellow pepper
I small fennel head
100 g / 4 oz button mushrooms
4 spring onions
225 g / 8 oz firm white fish
100 g / 4 oz long grain rice
25 g / I oz butter
100 g / 4 oz large unpeeled cooked
   prawns
2 Oxo Italian Herb & Spice cubes
50 ml / 2 fl oz dry white vermouth
250 g can mussels in brine

I Remove the core and seeds from the pepper and thinly slice. Trim the root and stalk ends of the fennel and cut it into thin wedges. Wash, dry and slice the mushrooms. Slice the spring onions. Cut the fish into cubes, discarding any skin and bones.

2 Cook the rice following the packet instructions.

3 Meanwhile, heat the butter in a large frying pan and add the pepper, fennel and mushrooms. Cook, stirring, over medium-high heat until just beginning to brown.

4 Add the spring onions, fish and prawns to the pan. Continue to cook until the fish is just opaque.

5 Crumble the Italian Herb & Spice cubes into 300 ml / ½ pt boiling water and add to the pan with the vermouth. Reduce the heat to medium and simmer until the fish is cooked. Drain and rinse the mussels and add to the pan. Cook for a further 2–3 minutes.

6 Spoon the cooked rice into shallow bowls. Add the fish, vegetables and juices. Serve immediately.

O X O *Tip*
No vermouth? Use dry sherry or, at a pinch, dry white wine.

Easy Gourmet Food

Pan-fried Chicken and Apples

Serve with hot rice or mashed potatoes to accompany the generous fruity sauce. If you are cooking the chicken in a microwave, then do use a browning dish.

30 ml / 2 tbsp plain flour
2 Chicken Oxo cubes
5 ml / 1 tsp ground cinnamon
4 boneless chicken breasts
30 ml / 2 tbsp cider vinegar
60 ml / 4 tbsp redcurrant jelly
2 large red-skinned apples
10 ml / 2 tsp oil
15 g / ½ oz butter

1 Put the flour, one crumbled Chicken cube and the cinnamon in a large freezer bag and shake to coat the inside of the bag. Skin the chicken, if preferred, and add to the bag. Seal the opening and shake to coat the chicken with the seasoned flour.

2 Crumble the remaining Chicken cube into a measuring jug and add 150 ml / ¼ pt boiling water, the vinegar and redcurrant jelly. Stir to dissolve the jelly.

3 Cut each apple into eight wedges, removing and discarding the core.

4 Heat the oil and butter in a large, non-stick frying pan. Add the chicken and cook over a high heat, turning frequently, until it is golden brown on both sides.

5 Add the apple wedges. Pour the stock mixture over the chicken. Bring just to the boil, cover and reduce the heat to medium-low. Cook gently for 15 minutes or until the chicken is cooked and the sauce has thickened.

6 Serve the chicken garnished with the apple wedges and with the sauce spooned over the top.

Easy Gourmet Food

OXO Tip
Small, skinless turkey breast fillets are becoming more popular and could easily be used in this recipe.

25 mins

Turkey in Coconut Sauce

Delicious served with tiny new potatoes

1 medium onion
3 medium carrots
550 g / 1¼ lb turkey breast
5 ml / 1 tsp oil
2 Chicken Oxo cubes
227 g can pineapple slices in natural
 juice
freshly ground pepper
75 g / 3 oz creamed coconut
15 g / ½ oz butter
a pinch of ground cinnamon

1 Peel and finely chop the onion. Peel and finely slice the carrots. Cut the turkey into bite-size pieces.

2 Heat the oil in a large non-stick frying pan. Add the onion and cook over medium heat until soft and golden brown, stirring frequently.

3 Add the turkey and cook until brown on all sides, turning occasionally. Stir in the carrots.

4 Dissolve the Chicken cubes in 150 ml / ¼ pt boiling water and add the juice from the can of pineapple. Add to the turkey and season with pepper.

5 Bring to the boil, cover and simmer gently for 15 minutes until the turkey is tender, stirring occasionally.

6 Roughly chop the coconut. Add to the pan and stir until melted.

7 In a separate non-stick frying pan, heat the butter until melted and sprinkle in the cinnamon. Add the pineapple and cook over a medium-high heat until lightly browned on both sides. Serve with the turkey.

OXO Tip

Boned and skinned chicken breasts would be equally good in place of the turkey. Look for blocks of creamed coconut among the oriental foods in the supermarkets – tightly wrap and refrigerate the unused portion.

Easy Gourmet Food

30 mins

Turkey and Artichoke Pie

Microwave the filling for this luscious pie if you wish, but once you have added the topping, bake it conventionally in the oven, so that it will be nice and crisp.

I Chicken Oxo cube
450 g / 1 lb turkey breast fillets
400 g can artichoke hearts
50 g / 2 oz butter
15 ml / 1 tbsp plain flour
75 ml / 3 fl oz double cream
freshly ground pepper
30 ml / 2 tbsp snipped chives
I Oxo Italian Herb & Spice cube
5 sheets filo pastry each measuring
about 30.5 x 23 cm / 12 x 9 in

1 Crumble the Chicken cube into 300 ml / ½ pt boiling water. Cut the turkey fillets into bite-sized cubes. Drain the artichokes and cut each in half.

2 Heat half the butter in a non-stick frying pan, add the turkey and cook over high heat, stirring constantly, until golden brown. Remove with a slotted spoon.

3 Remove the pan from the heat and blend the flour into the butter remaining in the pan. Gradually stir in the chicken stock until smooth. Return to the heat and cook, stirring constantly, until the sauce boils and thickens.

4 Remove from the heat and stir in the cream, a little pepper and the chives. Stir in the turkey, with any juices, and the artichoke hearts. Spoon into a pie dish.

5 Melt the remaining butter in a saucepan and stir in the crumbled Italian Herb & Spice cube.

6 Cut a sheet of filo pastry in half. Lightly brush the pieces with the seasoned butter, lightly crumple and place, buttered side uppermost, on top of the pie. Repeat with the remaining pastry sheets, making sure that the filling is covered. Drizzle over any remaining butter.

7 Bake at 200°C / 400°F / mark 6 for 20 minutes until golden brown. Serve immediately.

OXO Tip
Filo pastry is quite delicate – so handle it with care. Always keep the sheets you are not working with covered with a damp tea-towel to stop them drying out and becoming brittle.

Pan-fried Duck with Orange and Ginger Sauce

4 boned duck breasts
2 Oxo Chinese Herb & Spice cubes
1 medium orange
60 ml / 4 tbsp ginger preserve
5 ml / 1 tsp cornflour
30 ml / 2 tbsp red wine vinegar

1 Cut the duck lengthways into thin slices. Crumble over the Chinese Herb & Spice cubes and toss to coat the duck strips well. Cover and marinate in the refrigerator for 1 hour.

2 Finely grate the orange rind. Cut off the white pith. Cut the orange into segments.

3 Mix the orange rind with the ginger preserve, cornflour, vinegar and 150 ml / ¼ pt water.

4 Heat a large non-stick frying pan and add the duck in a single layer. Cook over a medium-high heat until the duck is crisp and brown on both sides. Lift out on to kitchen paper and keep warm.

5 Pour off the excess fat from the pan, retaining the juices. Add the orange and ginger mixture to the pan. Bring to the boil, mixing the pan juices into the sauce, and bubble gently for 1–2 minutes until the sauce is slightly syrupy. Gently stir in the orange segments.

6 Serve the hot sauce immediately with the duck.

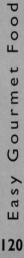

Easy Gourmet Food

Beef and Pepper Stroganoff

1 large onion
2 garlic cloves
1 large red pepper
450 g / 1 lb rump steak
1 Original Oxo cube
15 ml / 1 tbsp tomato purée
freshly ground pepper
10 ml / 2 tsp oil
5 ml / 1 tsp sugar
150 ml / ¼ pt soured cream

1 Peel and slice the onion thinly. Peel and chop the garlic finely. Remove the core and seeds from the peppers. Cut into thick slices. Cut the steak across the grain into thin slices.

2 Crumble the Original Oxo cube into 150 ml / ¼ pt boiling water and stir in the tomato purée. Season with pepper.

3 Heat the oil in a large non-stick frying pan. Add the steak and cook over a high heat, stirring constantly, until browned. Lift out of the pan.

4 Add the onion to the pan, sprinkle it with the sugar and cook over a medium heat until soft and golden. Add the garlic and pepper. Cook for 1 minute and then return the meat to the pan with any juices.

5 Pour over the stock and bring to a simmer. Cover and cook for 10 minutes.

6 Stir in the soured cream and heat through.

Easy Gourmet Food

30 mins

Lamb Biryani

To make a traditional Biryani (or Biriani), rice is layered with meat or vegetables and stock, and then baked in the oven or cooked very gently on the hob. In this speedy version the rice is cooked separately and mixed with the lamb and its sauce before serving.

I medium and I small onion
I garlic clove
350 g / 12 oz lean lamb
15 g / I oz whole blanched almonds
15 ml / 3 tsp oil
150 ml / ¼ pt natural yogurt
15 ml / I tbsp lemon juice
3 Oxo Indian Herb & Spice cubes
100 g / 4 oz basmati rice
15 ml / I tbsp flaked almonds
25 g / I oz sultanas, to garnish

1 Peel and roughly chop the medium onion. Peel and finely slice the small onion. Peel the garlic. Cut the lamb into bite-size cubes.

2 Put the chopped onion, garlic and whole almonds into a blender or food processor with 30 ml / 2 tbsp water. Process until a smooth purée is formed.

3 Heat 5 ml / 1 tsp oil in a large non-stick frying pan and quickly brown the lamb on all sides. Lift out with a slotted spoon.

4 Add another 5 ml / 1 tsp oil to the pan and cook the onion purée over a medium heat for about 3 minutes until golden brown, stirring frequently.

5 Stir in the yogurt, lemon juice and 50 ml / 2 fl oz water. Crumble in 2 Indian Herb & Spice cubes and stir in the lamb.

6 Bring just to the boil, cover and simmer gently for 20 minutes until the lamb is tender, stirring occasionally.

7 Meanwhile, cook the rice following packet instructions. Drain well.

8 Heat the remaining oil in a small non-stick frying pan and add the sliced onion. Crumble over the remaining Indian Herb & Spice cube and stir to coat the onion well. Cook over a medium heat until the onion begins to brown. Add the flaked almonds and continue cooking until the nuts and onions are golden brown.

9 Gently stir the rice into the lamb mixture. Sprinkle over the onion mixture and sultanas before serving.

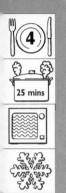

Pork in Sweet and Sour Sauce

Serve with rice or noodles.

227 g can pineapple slices in fruit juice
2 Oxo Chinese Herb & Spice cubes
30 ml / 2 tbsp tomato purée
45 ml / 3 tbsp red wine vinegar
45 ml / 3 tbsp soft brown sugar
30 ml / 2 tbsp cornflour
1 medium onion
1 garlic clove
2 large celery sticks
450 g / 1 lb pork fillet (tenderloin)
15 ml / 1 tbsp oil
freshly ground pepper
1 medium green pepper

1 Drain the pineapple, reserving the juice, and cut the slices in half. Make up the pineapple juice to 300 ml / ½ pt with water. Crumble in the Chinese Herb & Spice cubes and whisk in the tomato purée, vinegar, sugar and cornflour.

2 Peel and thinly slice the onion. Peel and crush the garlic. Finely slice the celery. Thinly slice the pork.

3 Heat the oil in a non-stick frying pan and add the onion, garlic and celery. Cook over a medium-high heat for about 3 minutes until soft, stirring occasionally.

4 Add the pork and cook for about 3 minutes until brown, stirring constantly. Season with pepper. Pour the sauce over the pork and bring to the boil, stirring.

5 Simmer gently for 10–15 minutes until the pork is tender, stirring occasionally.

6 Meanwhile, cut the pepper in half. Remove the core and seeds, then finely slice the flesh. Add the pepper and pineapple to the pork, cover and cook for 2–3 minutes until heated through.

OXO Tip

Try this dish using sliced chicken breast in place of pork – just as delicious.

Easy Gourmet Food

Stuffed Pork
with Baby Vegetables and Gravy

This is a colourful dish for a dinner party. The pork fillet can be stuffed and refrigerated in advance. If you wish to freeze the dish, then do so at the end of step 7 (before you add the fromage frais).

25 g / 1 oz butter
4 large fresh sage leaves
50 g / 2 oz fresh breadcrumbs
grated rind and juice of ½ lemon
salt and freshly ground pepper
450 g / 1 lb pork fillet (tenderloin)
50 g / 2 oz no-soak dried pitted prunes
5 ml / 1 tsp oil
16 baby carrots or 4 medium carrots
700 g / 1½ lb small new potatoes
2 Chicken Oxo cubes
200 g / 7 oz fromage frais

1 To make the stuffing, melt the butter in a small saucepan. Finely chop the sage leaves. Mix together the breadcrumbs, lemon rind and juice, sage, butter and seasoning.

2 Insert a sharp knife along the length of the pork fillet, cutting only two-thirds of the way through. Open it out and place between two sheets of greaseproof paper. Beat the fillet to flatten it slightly.

3 Spread the stuffing over the cut side of the pork and arrange the prunes down the centre. Roll up and tie securely in several places.

4 Heat the oil in a large non-stick frying pan and cook the pork for about 10 minutes, turning frequently, until brown on all sides.

5 If the carrots are medium size, cut each one into four sticks. Scatter the potatoes around the pork and put the carrots on top of the potatoes. Dissolve the Chicken cubes in 300 ml / ½ pt boiling water and add to the pan.

6 Bring to the boil, cover and simmer gently for about 30 minutes, until the vegetables are tender and the pork is cooked through.

7 Lift out the pork and vegetables on to a serving dish and keep warm.

8 Bring the pan juices to the boil to reduce them slightly. Whisk in the fromage frais and bring to the boil, stirring. Serve separately.

OXO Tip
Try using no-soak dried apricots instead of prunes in this recipe.

Index

American-style meatloaf with tomato sauce 64
Aubergine parmigiana 96

Bacon chops with mushroom sauce 41
Baked chilli peppers 34
Beans, creamy, with Parmesan toasts 106
Beef:
  pasta bake, Greek 50
  and pepper stroganoff 121
  carbonade of 46
  casserole, chilli 52
  pie, Somerset 48
  salad, oriental 88
  with peppers, sizzling spicy 10
Bombay potatoes 31

Carbonade of beef 46
Cheese burgers 68
Chicken:
  and apples, pan-fried 114
  and asparagus pasta 14
  and bacon salad, Italian 16
  and noodle soup, Chinese 19
  and tarragon soup 80
  and vegetable stir fry 18
  creole 42
  in apricot curry sauce 57
  Mexican, with fresh tomato salsa 82
  nuggets with two sauces, crisp 70
  tandoori 84
  with lemon and parsley garnish, Provençal 78
Chilli beef casserole 52
Chinese chicken and noodle soup 19
Chinese noodles with omelette rolls 30
Courgette risotto 94
Creamy beans with Parmesan toasts 106
Crisp chicken nuggets with two sauces 70

Deep-pan pizza 74
Duck, pan-fried, with orange and ginger sauce 120

Fish:
  quick spiced 23
  with lemon sauce, fried 22
Flash-fry steaks with sherried mushrooms 12
Fragrant Chinese meatballs 40
Frankfurter and potato hash, spicy 72
Fried fish with lemon sauce 22

Golden topped pork and butterbean bake 60
Greek beef and pasta bake 50

Honey glazed ribs 69

Indian plaice and spinach rolls 85
Italian chicken and bacon salad 16

Jacket potatoes with mustard sausage topping 32

Lamb:
  biryani 122
  casserole with herb dumplings, spring 54
  hotpot, spiced 56
  pasticcio 26

Lentil and carrot burgers 66

Meatballs:
  fragrant Chinese 40
  with minted yogurt, Turkish 90
Meatloaf, American-style, with tomato sauce 64
Mexican chicken with fresh tomato salsa 82
Moroccan vegetable couscous 108

Oriental beef salad 88

Pan-fried chicken and apples 114
Pan-fried duck with orange and ginger sauce 120
Peppers, baked 34
Pizza, deep-pan 74
Plaice and spinach rolls, Indian 85
Pork:
  amadine 8
  and butterbean bake, golden topped 60
  in sweet and sour sauce 124
  stuffed, with baby vegetables and gravy 126
Potatoes:
  Bombay 31
  with mustard sausage topping, jacket 32
Provençal chicken with lemon and parsley
    garnish 78

Quick spiced fish 23

Rainbow pasta 73
Ravioli Parmesan 100
Ribs, honey glazed 69
Risotto, courgette 94

Sausage goulash 38
Seafood primavera 112
Sizzling spicy beef with peppers 10
Somerset beef pie 48
Spiced lamb hotpot 56
Spicy frankfurter and potato hash 72
Spring lamb casserole with herb dumplings 54
Steaks, flash-fry, with sherried mushrooms 12
Stuffed pork with baby vegetables and gravy 126
Summer tortilla 86
Summer vegetable pie 36

Tandoori chicken 84
Tex-mex pasta 13
Tofu with sweet pepper sauce 98
Tuna and pasta bake 28
Turkey:
  and artichoke pie 118
  cassoulet 58
  escalopes with orange and rosemary 20
  in coconut sauce 116
Turkish meatballs with minted yogurt 90

Vegetable:
  chow mein 102
  curry 104
  pie, summer 36

White bean and mushroom soup 105